A Lion Guide

*Millhill Parish Church*

# A Death in the Family

Jean Richardson          *Pub 1979.*

**LION PUBLISHING**

LION PUBLISHING
Icknield Way, Tring, Herts

First edition 1979

ISBN 0 85648 114 9

Text set in 10/11pt Souvenir Light; printed in Great
Britain by Sir Joseph Causton & Sons Ltd, London &
Eastleigh

**Acknowledgements**
Illustrations by Kathy Wyatt and Ron Ferns
Cover photograph: Syndication International Ltd.
Photograph on page 9 by Sylvester Jacobs; on page 12 Fritz Fankhauser;
on page 30 CTVC, Bushey, Watford, from their documentary film *The Life
that's Left.*
Engraving on page 29 Mary Evans Picture Library.

The following books have been helpful in the preparation of this book: C.
Murray Parkes, *Bereavement,* Pelican; Sarah Morris, *Grief and how to live
with it,* Allen & Unwin; Katie Wiebe, *Alone,* Marshall, Morgan & Scott; C. S.
Lewis, *A Grief Observed,* Faber & Faber; Anne Hopkinson, *Families Without
Fathers,* Mothers Union

Some additional information and text by Rosemary A. Crewe have been
incorporated. The quotation on page 31 is from C. S. Lewis, *A Grief
Observed,* Faber & Faber.

# Contents

# Introduction

Death has suddenly become personal; it has hit where it hurts most, and you find you have to live the rest of your life without someone you loved.

This book has been written to help with the practical questions, emotional problems, spiritual matters—how to arrange a funeral, deal with a will, understand your irritability, let a room, find a job, and everything in between. There are also sections on grief and mourning to help you understand why you feel as you do, and what you can do to help yourself and those around you through this difficult time.

## Security

Bereavement snatches away our most basic human security. Our world crumbles, and we fall to our knees. The way in which we handle a crisis such as this depends much on our attitudes and beliefs. Personally, as a Christian, I could not have survived being widowed without the presence and strength of God, the prayers of fellow Christians and the support of friends.

## Make or break

An experience of such depth and magnitude as the death of a member of our family can either make or break us; it can destroy us, or it can mark a growing-point which leads to a new beginning. Death is part of life and it cannot be avoided; some time or other in life everyone comes face to face with it. It is always unexpected, always unwelcome and always causes pain.

With the pain come all sorts of other symptoms, and they usually follow a pattern—almost like an illness. As with an illness, with care and help, we recover, but while the illness lasts we see no end to it. Such is bereavement.

No two people come through it the same. I lost my husband fourteen years ago, and since then five other close members of my family have also died. And so I have come to understand a little more clearly the meaning of grief and how little prepared most of us are to cope with it.

I was already a Christian before my husband's death and the family had close connections with our local parish church. Bereavement put our faith to many tests, but it survived them all. Our shared experience has drawn us all closer to each other, although we are all now separated, physically.

In this book, I have drawn heavily on personal experience of the problems and difficulties—as well as some of the unexpected compensations—of widowhood and bringing up a family single-handed.

### About the author

Jean Richardson's husband died suddenly and unexpectedly in 1965. Her three sons were then 8, 13 and 16 years old. Not wanting to take a full-time job while they were still at school, she became a freelance writer. She has written and spoken widely on the subjects of bereavement and one-parent families, and has become well known as a regular broadcaster in *Prayer for the Day, Woman's Hour* and other BBC programmes.

# The first few days

When someone we love dies, particularly someone on whom we have depended, one of our strongest emotions is likely to be sheer panic. We feel helpless. We don't know what to do. Dimly, we are aware that 'arrangements' will have to be made but we don't know what they are or how to go about them.

The first step is to call the doctor. 'What must I do?' I asked my doctor when he told me my husband was dead. 'Nothing at all for an hour or two,' he said, 'I'll send people to help you.' Later that morning, the undertaker and the Rector of our church came and guided me through the decisions and arrangements which had to be made.

# The death

## Legal formalities

First of all, it is necessary to have the death certificate. The doctor or the hospital will issue this: It enables you to go ahead with the arrangements. If the body is to be cremated, the certificate will need the signatures of two doctors—this is purely a formality and does not mean there was anything suspicious about the death itself. Once the certificate has been issued, the death must be registered. This is usually done by the next of kin but a relative, executor or friend can take it along to the Registry Office and supply any other details which may be necessary.

## The next step

With the aid of the certificate of registration of death you can now claim

The death must be registered at the local office of the Registrar of Births, Marriages and Deaths within 5 days. He will need details of the dead person's previous occupation and age as well as a Certificate of Death—issued by a hospital doctor or GP. The registrar will give you a copy of the entry he makes in the register, a disposal certificate (so that you can proceed with funeral arrangements), and a copy of the Certificate of Registration of Death, Form BD 8. It is a good idea to ask for a couple of extra copies of this form to use when you claim allowances and insurance payments.

the various benefits that you ought to have. Brief details are given here, but leaflets and advice are readily available.

## Announcing the death

Some undertakers supply printed cards for you to send out or enclose in personal letters to tell people what has happened. The undertaker will also arrange for any announcements to be inserted in local or national newspapers and, if necessary, help you with the wording of these.

I am always sorry when I read in such announcements the words 'No letters'. Just at first, letters can be a burden rather than a comfort, but even those who feel they can't face them at the time often regret their decision later on. They can always be put on one side—or

### Benefits and allowances

DEATH GRANT of up to £30 is paid to the next of kin, executor or person who pays for funeral. Apply to your local social-security office within 6 months. For more information see their leaflet number NI49.
WIDOW'S ALLOWANCE is paid to most widows for the first 26 weeks of widowhood. Claim from a social-security office on form BW1 within 3 months. The current weekly rate is £27.30 plus an earnings-related allowance.
WIDOWED MOTHER'S ALLOWANCE is paid after the widow's allowance ceases to widows with one or more children under 19 living at home. The current payment of £19.50 (plus £5.35 for each child) a week is usually paid automatically.
WIDOW'S PENSION is paid (usually automatically) to widows of 40 or over without dependent children. The amount varies from £5.85 to £19.50 a week (depending on your age).
WIDOWERS do not receive benefit.

answered by another member of the family—and can be an unexpected source of pride and comfort after the worst of the grief has subsided.

Bereaved children will almost certainly want to know, when they are older, what friends, colleagues and relatives wrote about their dead parent, while people outside the family usually welcome this opportunity to express their sympathy and sense of loss.

# The funeral

The first step is to get in touch with an undertaker; he will then take charge of everything. He will need to know whether the service is to take place in church or at a crematorium and whether the dead person is to be buried or cremated. The undertaker will then consult the clergyman and/or the

**burial**

gravestone is a permanent memorial

symbolizes being laid to rest

follows biblical tradition

**but**

burial is very costly

grave needs tending

**cremation**

much cheaper than burial

symbolizes purifying release

ecologically sound—saves land for
   the living

no grave to look after

**but**

some dislike the idea of being burned

historically has pagan associations

often no visible memorial

Funeral costs vary greatly, according to how elaborate the funeral is and where it takes place (London is the most expensive). The funeral director always pays fees on behalf of his clients and his bill covers most aspects of the funeral, e.g. church service, burial or cremation, hire of hearse and car, notification cards, etc. Check exactly what is covered when you ask for an estimate of funeral costs. The cost will be £150 at the very least.

crematorium and suggest the day and time when the funeral can take place. He will want to know how many cars will be needed, if there are to be flowers, whether you want to follow the hearse from the house or meet it at the door of the church or crematorium.

Even if there is to be no church service, the undertaker will normally notify the local clergyman so that he can visit the bereaved family before the funeral and also a few weeks later, when the mourners may be feeling the full force of what has happened.

## The church service

The actual form of the service will depend on the denomination of the church where the funeral takes place. Traditionally, the minister meets the procession at the door and the coffin is carried in, followed by the mourners, who sit together in the front few pews. In some places, it is now the custom for the coffin to be brought to the church a little before the service and for the mourners to take their places as they arrive, rather than to follow the coffin in

procession. You may be asked which arrangement you would prefer. In either case the mourners follow the coffin out of the church at the end of the service before the rest of the congregation leaves.

The undertaker will already have asked if all the mourners are to go on to the burial ground or the crematorium or whether only the men or immediate family intend to do so. He will also have arranged for cars to take the mourners to the final ceremony and to the house where they will meet when it is all over.

## Music

Most church services include music. Often, a hymn which was a favourite of the dead person is sung, but, if you are not sure which to choose, the clergy will usually be able to suggest one or two. Funeral hymns need not always be slow and sad—the Christian hope is that there is new life *after* death and this positive approach can be reflected in brighter hymns than are often considered suitable for this occasion. There will generally be an organist to provide any music you may choose but it is not usual for the choir to attend unless specially asked for, except sometimes when the dead person was a prominent member of the church or community.

A short address may be given during the service recalling the life of the dead person, but many clergy now feel that this only adds to the strain for the family. They prefer to use the prayers to thank God for his/her character and example, to commit him/her to God's love and to ask for comfort and peace for those who mourn.

## The crematorium service

This is a shortened form of the church service and can include music and hymns if desired. It can be conducted either by your local clergyman or by the chaplain attached to the crematorium. The coffin is placed on a sliding belt while the prayers and words of committal are said and then it slips gently through a door or curtains.

Any flowers or wreaths will have been placed in a small area outside the chapel where the mourners can see them after the service and read the cards; the flowers will remain there for a few days.

## Disposal of the body

If the funeral service in church is to be followed by burial, the mourners will be taken to the burial ground for the final, very short, committal ceremony at the grave. From there, they will return to the house or else go their way, according to the arrangements they have made.

Most graves, these days, are marked by a simple headstone which can be erected any time after two months or so, once the ground has settled. More elaborate memorials will have to wait for nine to twelve months.

If the body was cremated, the urn containing the ashes can be buried in the area of the cemetery reserved for this. This can be done as soon as the simple memorial plaque is ready, and the short committal follows a similar pattern to the burial of a body. The practice of planting a rose tree alongside the plaque makes these quiet places in the churchyard or burial ground beautiful and hopeful to visit later.

Alternatively, you can arrange for the ashes to be scattered. This normally takes place in the crematorium Garden of Remembrance from one to fourteen days after the cremation. You can choose to be present if you wish.

## Significance of the funeral

Every bereaved person dreads this ordeal, but, whatever form this final ceremony takes, from a psychological point of view it is most important. Even quite young children should be included in this public act of mourning.

The funeral helps to impress the fact that death *has* taken place and the need to come to terms with what has happened. Much comfort is drawn from the gathering together of family, friends and neighbours. It brings home the reality of the situation when the mind is still numb enough to be protected from all the implications. The funeral marks the end of a brief period where all seems unreal, and is an essential part of mourning.

## Coping with grief

An understanding doctor will, if asked, give you something to help you through the day but it is unwise to expect any drug to be anything more than a temporary solution. After the death of her husband, radio personality Lady Barnett said, 'Widows should be allowed to experience the grief of losing their husbands and widowers their wives without being treated with sleeping-pills and tranquillizers.' She is sure that it is better for anyone who mourns to get grief out of the system while everyone around is being kind and helpful.

I myself feel it is better to live through a time of misery and sadness with a relatively clear head and as much dignity as one can muster, trying to realize that some aspects of life *are* tragic and have to be accepted. Most people would recover their balance and composure more quickly if doctors and well-meaning relatives would allow them to be thoroughly miserable for a time. This is the normal and healing reaction to sorrow and loss.

However upsetting it may be to other people to see the distress of mourners at a funeral, they should try to see also that grief and tears are natural and be glad that nature is taking a hand in the healing process.

Many people find a cup of tea particularly comforting. The body loses moisture through crying, so it is good to drink more than usual. Don't be afraid to take an aspirin if you get a headache from the tension—they won't cause any dependence. The more you take care of your physical needs, the fewer problems you will have.

# The will

As soon as possible after the death, those appointed to be responsible for the distribution of the dead person's belongings, known in legal language as the executors, should get together. They should arrange to see a solicitor and ask him to obtain probate. This is the legal name for transferring all the dead person's property to them, so that they can then distribute it on the dead person's behalf. This process is known as 'proving a will' and should not take more than a few weeks, depending on how complicated or how simple the will is, and on how fast the solicitor works.

## The solicitor

The choice of solicitor is up to the executors, and they should ask him for a rough estimate of his fees before engaging him to do the job. If the executors are not satisfied with the amount, they are quite at liberty to shop around.

Solicitors are there to help you, and

will answer any queries you may have in terms which you will understand. They will tell you that no part of the dead person's estate (everything that he/she owned) can be distributed until the will has been 'proved'. They will explain what this means and how it affects you.

## No will

They will also help you if you find that the person has, as far as you can see, died without making a will. This is termed 'intestacy'. In this situation the relatives should gather together all the information they can about what the person owned, his estate, and take all the documents they can find to the solicitor. There are certain rules laid down by law to cover intestacy, and usually the husband or wife will inherit the estate.

## A do-it-yourself will

Sometimes the dead person will have made his will without the help of a solicitor, usually on a form obtained from a stationer. In this case the executors, if there are any, should take the will to a solicitor as soon as possible after the death, so that he can try to obtain probate. There are many legal pitfalls which someone making his own will may have fallen into, so it is always advisable to go to a solicitor when you want to make a will (see page 62).

## A disputed will

If you (or any close relative of the dead person) feel that you have been treated unfairly in the will, you should write to the solicitor and tell him this as soon as possible. You may find that you can appeal to the court for the will to be changed in your favour, but you must

lodge your complaint within six months of probate being granted.

## How long?

So long as there are not too many complications, an estate can usually be wound up within six months of the death. When a business is involved it may take longer. The cost varies considerably, and will, of course, depend on how long it takes the solicitor to sort it all out. His fee will usually come out of the estate.

## Belongings

One of the most difficult tasks to tackle after a death is the disposal of the dead person's clothes and effects. It is best done as soon as possible. If you can't face it alone, ask a member of the family or a close friend to help you with it. The longer you put it off, the more you will dread it and it will be at the back of your mind all the time.

At all costs, resist the temptation to 'make a shrine' of the room or chair or workbench. A century ago, it was a common custom to leave everything as it had been, to behave as though the dead person would be coming back and to try to maintain a relationship which no longer existed. Many lives have been cramped and stunted by this attitude to death. By all means keep and treasure some things which have special significance and provide *happy* memories, but best give the rest away.

There will be some items which you may want certain people to have, such as a piece of jewellery or a fountain pen, which you know they will treasure too and keep as a memento. Of the remainder, clothing, books or furniture are always needed by various voluntary organizations who will usually arrange for them to be collected.

# Understanding death

## What is death?

Nothing perplexes people more than death. It seems a strange, unnatural disaster that makes us aware we have no power, in the end, to control our own life. What does it mean? Why should it happen? How can we best face up to it?

## The body dies

Looked at medically, there is nothing unnatural about death. Throughout life the parts of the body continually repair themselves, but as we get older these repairs are not as successful as they used to be, and at last the vital organs break down. Similarly the body's repair systems may not be able to cope when it is harmed by disease or severe injury. The heart stops beating, breathing ceases and—the final, irreversible step—the brain no longer functions. Then life has departed and cannot be brought back.

## More than a body

It is hard to believe that when the body dies the person no longer exists, though some think so. Despite the mystery of death, most people find it rings true that the human personality is more than just the body and that in some way we must pass through death. There have been many different beliefs about what actually happens. Some have thought that man has an immortal soul which at death is freed from the hindrances of the body. Some believe that the dying person is taken into God and merged with the divine, losing his identity. Hinduism and other eastern faiths teach reincarnation—that after death people are re-born as another baby or an animal, and so on over and over again.

## A whole person

Christians believe that we are more than just bodies. But we are not immortal spirits living in our bodies like snails in

### Biblical statements about death

If our hope in Christ is good for this life only and no more, then we deserve more pity than anyone else in all the world. But the truth is that Christ has been raised from death, as the guarantee that those who sleep in death will also be raised.

Our brothers, we want you to know the truth about those who have died, so that you will not be sad, as are those who have no hope. We believe that Jesus died and rose again, and so we believe that God will take back with Jesus those who have died believing in him.

Jesus said to Martha, 'I am the resurrection and the life. Whoever believes in me will live, even though he dies; and whoever lives and believes in me will never die.'

their shells, so that at death we can discard the useless body with relief. We are whole people, a unity of body and spirit. My body is me, not a shell; my personality is expressed through my body.

## Separation

So there *is* something unnatural about death. It separates the personality from the body, which were meant to be closely joined. And, as the bereaved know only too well, death separates you from those you love. The anguish and horror of death show that it is an enemy of mankind. The Bible makes sense of all this by explaining that death is the result of mankind's disobeying God and ignoring him. It is the final stage in a separation even worse than the others—the separation of each of us from God. That is a kind of 'death' even while we're alive.

## New life in Jesus

So Christians look at death realistically and don't try to say it doesn't matter. They recognize how dreadful it is. They realize we also have a source of hope—Jesus Christ, who was executed on a cross but who was raised back to life by God. Everyone who trusts in him can have the assurance that after death he will be with Jesus. Because Jesus died for us, we need no longer be separated from God. And when he rose again from death it was to a new life in which we too can share. Because that new life is imperishable, death is now a gateway to an even closer friendship with God. It is a deep comfort to those left behind to know that death can't separate them for ever from those who have died, because in Christ they will be reunited.

## The resurrection of the body

The Christian idea of heaven is not a place where immortal souls float around! Although death does separate the personality from the body for a time, in Jesus they will be joined again. After all, Jesus himself was raised from death physically, with a real body, not as a ghost. Christians believe that when this world's time is up, the bodies of all who have died will be raised. We shall be judged by God as whole people, and believers will have an unimaginably full life with God for ever.

## No longer unbearable

And so death loses its terror for those who believe the Christian good news. It is still solemn, and undeniably sad, but our hope makes it bearable. This isn't wishful thinking, either, for it is based on God's strength and love which he had demonstrated by raising Jesus.

# Realization

# Death of a parent

When a parent dies, we nearly always experience feelings of guilt and remorse. We reproach ourselves for not appreciating them more when they were alive, for not visiting them more often, for not doing more to help them. We remember our unkindness or impatience.

If Grandma or Grandpa had grown difficult with age and were living with us in a small house, we may remember the times we half-wished they'd die or that someone else would look after them. Now that this wish has been granted, we may torment ourselves with regret. We wish we could call them back and say, 'I didn't mean it'.

Many sons, going back to the room or house where a parent had passed the final years of life, realize with shame what a difference another coat of paint

would have made and how little time it would have taken to do.

## In proportion

It is important to realize that such regrets are natural and that the dead parent may well have felt impatience, annoyance and exasperation with *us*. Family life includes conflict as well as love. We have to accept remorse as part of our mourning, not glossing over past attitudes but not giving them greater significance than they deserve.

There will have been faults on both sides, and in earlier days, under less trying circumstances, no doubt both people would have flared up, calmed down and even had a good laugh over the very things which just now strike us as unforgivable. Such emotions will, of course, go all the deeper and be more tormenting in the rare cases where the dead person has committed suicide.

## God's forgiveness

The Christian response to distressing memories of things done and left undone is to offer up our conflicting emotions to God, our heavenly Father. He knows our temperaments and family characteristics and what the pressures were. We can thank him for our parents and all they did for us; we can remember the good times and ask forgiveness for the bad, reminding ourselves that the love which enables us to make allowances for our own children is a reflection of *his* love which understands and forgives *us*.

While people are still alive, there is always time to put things right, but death is final and robs us of that opportunity. But if, when they are no longer with us, we now think only with love towards the person we have neglected or misunderstood, and if we can learn from our experience to do everything we can for those who *are* still with us, then gradually these feelings of guilt will lessen and we shall be comforted.

## Helping others

Many old people today live alone and far away from their families. Many of them would enjoy better health and spirits if they could be included in the activities of another family near at hand. Helping others is a sure way of helping ourselves, and many people whose own parents have died find satisfaction in befriending a lonely grandparent or a single person and involving them in their normal family life.

# Death of a child

This is one of the most bitter forms of bereavement. It seems all wrong, unnatural and, for the child, completely undeserved. A real part of ourselves has been torn from us.

## Real love

Much similar guilt and remorse will be felt, but again we need to remind ourselves that impatience, cross words, misunderstandings are all part of family life. Children know when genuine love exists. They soon recognize that it is love which prompts what may seem to them harsh or unjust behaviour on the part of parents.

Children see things in black and white and do not hold grudges. They thrive better on clashes where love is, than on indifference or total freedom to do as they like without love. One little girl arrived at school, sobbing bitterly. When the teacher asked her what was wrong, said, 'Mummy doesn't love me—she never says, "Mind the road!" '

## A valuable life

Although Christian parents will be as shattered by their child's death as anyone else, it is, I think, a *little* easier to accept because a belief in a future life gives a proportion and perspective to this one. We are all locked up in our ideas of time, but for God time is unimportant. This means that a short and, to our minds, tragically incomplete life is just as valid and valuable to him as one of seventy or eighty years.

The Compassionate Friends is an organization of bereaved parents. The society has many local branches and the national secretary can be contacted at 50 Woodwaye, Watford, Herts, WD1 4NW (Watford 24279).

## On loan

We all want what is best for those we love, but what *we* think is best for them may not always be in their long-term interest. If we believe that children are on loan from God, it becomes easier to understand that he loves them far more than we ever could, and will never let them slip from him. As events sometimes turn out, it may even become possible to be thankful that they were not called upon to face some disease or disaster which may have demanded more from them than they would have been able to give.

There is no glib or easy answer to the 'Why?' of the death of a child. Our reassurance must lie in the conviction that Jesus, who said 'Let the children come to me', will hold them in life and death and keep them safe.

## Safe for ever

Only God is perfect, so it isn't a surprise to realize that even children are spoiled by the wrongness of the world. They are weak, like everyone else, and as they grow older and more able to form their own opinions, they too have to establish their own values. The most important of these is to learn where God comes into our lives, and to love him. If we do love him, then to be with him, safe for ever, is the best thing we could ever wish for ourselves or our children. This is what Christians know as heaven.

In the baptism of our children we take on the responsibility of making decisions on their behalf. We promise to bring the children up in the Christian way. However, God is more concerned about our inward relationship with him than for the outward ceremony of baptism. We can be assured that all children are especially dear to God, who is Love.

## Brothers and sisters

If there are other children in the family, the parents must look beyond their own grief. Brothers and sisters will need comfort, strength, patience and more love than ever. They must not be excluded from the emotions which will hit them just as hard, though in different ways. It is important that the neighbourhood, shocked by bereavement, does not add to their burden by conveying a sense of isolation. This can lead to an unconscious shunning of the bereaved family, people feeling that they will want to be left alone, and so the children will feel more bewildered or shut out than ever. They must always be allowed to grieve with their parents within the security of the family circle.

# The still-born child

Many people think that a still-birth or the death of a baby a few days old does not cause the same grief as the loss of an older child. But the wounds are just as deep and painful. The bereaved mother should not be put in a ward with women nursing their live children but taken home as soon as medically possible to be comforted by relatives or friends and any other children she may have.

## Grief and fears

Many mothers of still-born children say that they have never 'got over' this experience. Times come when they re-live the disappointment and wonder what the child would now be like had he or she lived.

The father usually has to go back to work after a few days, leaving the mother at home, still weak and emotional. This is when support from neighbours and friends is most necessary. Usually, the mother's most pressing need will be to talk about what has happened. She may need to voice fears about her *next* baby being still-born; to express her feelings of guilt; that the doctors had let her down; even that, without a child to nurse, her health may suffer. The greatest help will be to lend a sympathetic but practical ear.

What about the father of a still-born child? His grief will be just as great and his frustrations perhaps greater. He has the knife-twisting duty of registering the death at the same time as the birth, and having to make arrangements which will spare the mother, such as putting away the baby clothes and the pram.

## Funeral

After any bereavement, the funeral is very important, even in the case of a very young child. Simply to take away the baby hinders rather than helps the parents to adjust to its death. Some parents are not even told what has happened to their baby. This can prolong their agony. Such insensitivity does unfortunately happen in some hospitals. The parents need to mourn their loss openly at a funeral ceremony. They need to grieve, letting the tears which heal bitterness flow while strength returns.

## Miscarriage or abortion

When a baby is growing inside the womb, the hormones, which are the body's chemical messengers, are telling the mother's body how to prepare for the birth. When this process is interrupted by the loss of the baby, the body is confused and takes a while to settle down.

During this time, you may well feel emotional and depressed. You may feel cheated out of having a baby and wonder why yours was lost. There is usually a very good reason for the body rejecting a baby before birth—often the baby is abnormal and might have grown up handicapped.

If you have chosen to have an abortion, you may have the added burden of feeling responsible for the death. This may be offset by the relief of not having an unwanted or a handicapped child, but at such a time feelings are inevitably mixed.

When you have lost a child in this way you may find yourself worrying about its spiritual future. One couple I know asked their minister to read the funeral service to them after a miscarriage and found this a great comfort.

# Death of husband or wife

Every married couple has to face the fact that sooner or later one of them will die. It is estimated that one woman in five will be a widow before she is 60. For most people, these facts are too disturbing, and so, when the inevitable happens, the shock is all the greater.

Whether or not you take the Christian view of marriage, it is a fact that husband and wife become bound to each other in far more subtle ways than being mere parties to a contract. When your husband or wife dies, life loses its centre so that you feel disorientated, off-balance, wounded. In his widely-read book, A Grief Observed, C. S. Lewis wrote, 'No one ever told me that grief felt so like fear.' What will happen? we ask ourselves. What shall we do? Who will care? And, unlike the death of a parent or a child, this is one experience we have to face alone. Only those who have been through the same experience can be expected to understand. For this reason, another widow or widower is probably the best person to turn to for help.

Suddenly you are back where you started—a single person but older than the last time round. Your marriage contract is ended; you must start a new life. The pangs of birth into this life will be there, but they will not last for ever, though at the time it may seem so. Do not be afraid to ask another man or woman to help you with the things your partner did in the marriage. If your husband always filled in your tax return there is sure to be a man you know who would be pleased to help you; or in the case of a widower, a woman who will be happy to mend a torn shirt.

## No easy way

Never think you are alone in feeling as you do or that 'it's different for some'. It is certainly no easier for the Christian. In some ways, bereavement is harder, because Christians often feel that they *should* be able to overcome these emotions. They then worry because they feel they are not coping as well as they should. But one aspect *is* different for the Christian—belief in a future life and in the never-ending love of God makes it easier for the Christian to 'let go' of the one they loved.

This 'letting go' is all-important. Without it, we shall never fully recover our serenity and will be left with a sense of deep hopelessness. Making a shrine of the dead person's room, visits made too often to the grave, shutting out other people and other interests from our lives—all such refusals to 'let go' stunt our growth and would certainly not be what our partner would want for us. If it is true that the scars of bereavement never entirely disappear, it is just as true that if we do not let our dead go, the wounds will not heal.

## Effective faith

In the early days, following my husband's death, I dreaded the nights. I found then, as in other crises since, that I couldn't pray. Instead, familiar words from the Bible kept running through my mind—'I will never leave you; I will never abandon you'; 'in quietness and in trust shall be your strength'.

I was so thankful, then, to have been brought up as a Christian—it seems to me that there can be no such thing as 'instant faith'; it has to be built up over the years slowly, until it imperceptibly becomes part of us. I've found that when life suddenly calls for the exercise of great faith, it's usually at a time when coherent thought—even prayer—is impossible. All I could ask was; 'Please don't let me be bitter.'

The question we have to put to ourselves is not the all-too-frequent 'Why should this happen to me?' but 'This happens to other people—why *shouldn't* it happen to me?' Death is universal; it comes to all and should never be thought of as a punishment from God. God does not exempt us from death by changing the natural laws which he himself has made. When he

became man as Jesus Christ, even he willingly accepted death for us, in order to destroy the power of death. The Christian promise is that as death could not hold him, so it does not have the final word over us or those we love.

# When a friend dies

It is often assumed that the 'worst' form of bereavement is the death of a husband or wife, but every bereavement is shattering in its own way.

The death of a friend brings a different but equally piercing sense of loss, especially in the case of two people who may have shared their lives since student days or in the case of homosexuals who may have lived together loyally all their adult lives. The effects of the broken relationship will in many ways be the same as for a widow or widower, and made even more poignant because there will usually be no children to help, and because others may think one's grief out of place.

We tend to underestimate a person's grief for a dead friend. Even when close friends have been physically separated for many years, there is grief for the loss of early shared experiences and all the close ties which still bind them together uniquely.

# Coping with grief

It is perfectly normal for a bereaved person to be sad, withdrawn and tearful. It does *not* mean that he or she is depressive or neurotic. Normal, human experiences are not merely medical problems to be cured with pills, though these may help. Grief is like an illness, though, and can be disabling. Sometimes it produces physical symptoms of its own, and it doesn't help to ignore it. No matter how 'sensible' we imagine ourselves to be, our emotional behaviour after the loss of someone close to us seems puzzling and frightening. It is possible to remain dry-eyed and apparently unmoved at the funeral and yet be undone by very little things.

# The pattern

After the first, numbing shock there comes a period of pining followed by mixed feelings of depression and apathy alternating with bursts of intense activity and, often, anger and despair.

## How long?

Many mourners have cried, 'How long will it last?' It is impossible to generalize. Within reason, any length of time is 'normal'. Such a fundamental adjustment has to be a gradual process. A rough estimate would be a year or two, while we learn to accept what has happened and to adapt to the situation. After, say, two years, a drawn-out, disabling grief suggests that medical help should be sought. Such a problem is familiar to a doctor and he will be able to help you over the depressive stage of your bereavement.

**Timetable of grief** (the stages and their order vary, and may overlap)

| | | |
|---|---|---|
| 1 | Shock | Muscular weakness, emptiness and inner tension |
| 2 | Numbness | Everything seems unreal and remote |
| 3 | Struggle between fantasy and reality | You find reality difficult to accept and may act partly as though it had not happened |
| 4 | Feelings of guilt, panic or frenzy | You may want to withdraw from the outside world and even your family |
| 5 | Depression | To be expected: for physical symptoms see page 23 |
| 6 | Release | Shedding of tears or release of a flood of grief |
| 7 | Painful memories | You find yourself able to face memories and accept them |
| 8 | Acceptance | Your new life begins and plans for the future form |
| | | Practical and emotional problems become easier to deal with |

If your children are in need of more support than you can give them at the moment, then the health visitor will also call, and perhaps your local-authority social worker. They will be able to advise on day nurseries or put you in touch with a registered child-minder.

## Working together

It is better to be occupied than to sit about and worry. It will help the children if they are allowed to give a hand with any job they can do. To do things together gives everyone a sense of purpose and security. In all times of grief, habit can be a comfort—to go *on* doing the daily chores, peeling the potatoes, going to work, and the like.

## Understanding yourself

No one who has not experienced bereavement can fully understand its conflicting emotions. It is like a second adolescence, with all the adolescent's swings of mood. You are over-sensitive to casual remarks; you dread waking up in the morning, especially at weekends when you imagine everyone else is having a good time. Everything becomes out of proportion: nothing seems as important as your own grief.

Most people discover that their restlessness comes from the instinct to look for the dead person; the hope that he or she hasn't really gone. One woman found herself needlessly re-arranging the airing cupboard and turning out drawers before she recognized her deep need to 'find' her dead husband. Some try to 'bring back' the loved one by way of fantasies or speaking aloud to them as though they were in the room. Some experience vivid dreams; many of these recall happy events in the past but most have an underlying uneasiness.

## Vivid memories

Equally common is the sharply-defined recollection of the events which led up to the death and the ability of the bereaved to recount every detail of the previous hours and days. It is as though time stood still just as a single moment is captured in a photograph.

You remember that it was the day the milkman was late or the day you missed the bus to work. One man, months later, was able to recite word for word a letter he had just read when the news of his wife's death was brought to him. Bereaved people will hang on to such details as a means of making their dead seem closer and still with them in the world.

## Finding your way

We react differently according to our temperament, our upbringing, the people we are with and other less obvious causes. Some long to talk to anyone who will listen; others shut themselves away and talk within themselves; others will write it all down in the form of a diary or a letter to the one who has died.

There is no 'right' way of grieving—everyone has to work a way through by whatever method brings most relief and comfort. Although we can derive much help and insight from other people's experiences, in the end we all have to fight our own way through the jungle, making use of every bit of encouragement we can find.

# What to expect

The trouble is—we don't know *what* to expect! Death has probably never before come so close. It is a new experience and we don't know how to deal with it. A book like this can help by trying to explain what is happening and describing the emotions which are tearing you apart. Whatever your emotions may be, never be afraid of your own reactions to grief. Accept them, understand them, and you will be half-way to using them positively.

## Numbness

Remind yourself that you are in a state of emotional shock. Be thankful for the numbness which carries you through the first days or weeks, even though you know that feeling is bound to return —like the pain in frost-bitten fingers when they begin to thaw.

If possible, use this short break, when often the mind works clearly and competently on a practical level, to cope with the immediate problems, and thus prevent yourself losing confidence in your ability to manage on your own. But you should try not to make any far-reaching decisions until later: in your present state of mind your judgement will not be reliable.

## The second stage

This is when many irrational fears and emotions come to the surface. These are entirely natural. People often feel physically ill, fear they are going mad or think they are about to have a nervous breakdown. As they struggle to control the conflict inside them, all sorts of dreadful possibilities run through their minds. None of these imaginary disasters is likely to happen. One of the greatest fears a young parent may have is that he or she will also die and leave the children orphaned. Dying of a 'broken heart' is not entirely unknown but it is extremely unlikely.

## Physical symptoms

Sometimes, physical symptoms will attack the bereaved; these normally fade within a week or so without producing the real illness from which the dead person had suffered. The day after my husband's funeral, I went to my doctor because one side of my face was swollen and inflamed and I was sure that I had 'caught' the same disease. The doctor assured me that I was perfectly healthy and that my face would soon return to normal. It did.

A young husband whose wife had died in pregnancy suffered for several days what could only be described as labour pains.

Many women who have lost a husband as a result of heart disease imagine that they are about to go the same way, not realizing that quickened heart-beats or palpitations are often the response to fear and anxiety.

The only thing which saves us from hypochondria is a sense of humour. Try to see the funny side of your reactions. I have thanked God for the laughter of family and friends.

## Anger

One emotion which upsets and shocks many people is a feeling of extreme anger. Anger frequently goes with fear; an animal may be docile until something frightens it, when it will turn and attack. For the bereaved person, the world has

---

Every bereaved person will experience some of the following physical and emotional symptoms:

| | |
|---|---|
| insomnia | nervousness |
| trembling | depression |
| coldness | panic |
| indigestion | anxiety |
| constipation | sweating |
| coughs and colds | fear of illness |
| lapses of memory | fear of breakdown |
| fatigue | headaches |
| loss of appetite | dizziness |
| lack of concentration | diarrhoea |
| itching skin | irritability |
| blurred vision | lack of interest |
| difficulty in swallowing | fullness in the throat |

suddenly become a very frightening place, and one reaction is to fight back. Most people blame themselves in some measure for the death of someone near to them, and because this is too painful to bear they tend to take it out on someone else.

A widow will find many scapegoats on which to unload her anger at what life has thrown at her. One woman marched into her husband's office and accused his colleagues of not pulling their weight and leaving him to shoulder all the responsibility. Another blamed her doctor for making what she considered was a wrong diagnosis.

## Grievance

There is often a deep sense of grievance. Life seems very unjust. Many blame God. 'How can he love us if he lets this happen?' they ask. 'What have we done to deserve this?' There is no need to feel guilty for voicing such thoughts. When doctors are the subject of wild accusations after bereavement, they do not let it affect their relationship with the patient. How much greater is God's understanding of our turmoil.

The greatest comfort we have is to know that we can take all our fears, resentment and anger to him, believing that such destructive emotions will dissolve in his love to be replaced by peace and hope. We don't become immune from tragedy if we believe in God, but we can be protected from bitterness and despair in our suffering by his strength and presence with us.

## Bitterness

Bitterness is a destructive emotion which we must guard against. If we become bitter it will set up hostilities within the family on account of the cruel, unjust things we shall say. This is a time when we should be drawing strength from being united, but, sadly, it can also be a time when relationships are damaged beyond repair.

It should not be necessary to point out that a child must never be blamed for contributing to the death of a parent or a brother or sister. That would be too much for him to bear when he is already suffering under his own burden of grief.

For the same reason, it is thoughtless as well as stupid to vent one's anger on a close friend or relative. They, too, have been bereaved and will be feeling angry; if a situation develops beyond control, lasting divisions can result. Not only that—if we persist in unreasonable anger and reproaches, we drive other people away and find ourselves more bereft than ever.

## Hallucination

Another disconcerting effect of bereavement is a form of hallucination in which we 'see' the dead person. This

**Destructive attitudes**
bitterness
despair
pride
shutting yourself away
self-pity
looking for someone to blame
becoming a martyr
cursing God

**Constructive attitudes**
accepting what has happened
hopefulness
faith in the future
making the most of what is left
willingness to recover
being thankful for the past
accepting help and friendship
committing everything to God

can be so vivid that we find ourselves reaching out to touch him or her. This, too, is normal and becomes less frequent. But it can be an agonizing disappointment to walk along a street, *sure* that the person in front is your

dead relative. It may be just a way of walking, but the jolt is enough to pierce the heart and bring back all the pain. Even after so long, it still happens to me and I can only turn to Jesus, who knew what sadness and grief are like.

# Letting them go

Letting go of our dead is the most difficult and yet the most important part of grief and mourning. Gradually we have to cut those ties which hold us back from making a new life for ourselves and the family. Memories must remain and be a source of comfort and thankfulness, but if we refuse to accept the fact of death we shall become stunted, unable to grow—surely this would not be what those who loved us would want to happen.

## Associations

Mercifully, the true realization of what we have lost comes only slowly, but each day will bring its reminders of the past. This pervading sadness was summed up by one widow who said, 'I keep thinking I must tell Jim about that when he gets home—and then I remember that I shan't be able to tell him anything ever again.'

Different associations bring pain to different people. A widower never set foot in his local pub after his wife died because they had always had their Saturday lunch there when she was alive. Another man wrote to his vicar and told him he intended joining another church because he felt he would always 'see' his wife in the pew they had always occupied, and he felt he must begin a new church life in a different building.

Although I can hardly believe now

that it took so long, my diary tells me that it was four years before I could listen to a record or go to a concert. I do remember, though, that the tears which accompanied the music when I did feel able to hear it again were peaceful rather than painful, and I knew that another stage of my own mourning had passed.

If you have lived with someone for a long time, it makes it all the more difficult to take decisions and make changes you know your partner would probably have disapproved of or disliked. There was a man I used to visit; his wife had recently died and his sons wanted him to have a television set. 'No,' he said, 'Emmy didn't approve of television.' Nothing would move him. Unfortunately, Emmy hadn't been too keen on the radio, either, so his evenings must have been long and lonely. However, in the end he *was* persuaded to have a set, though obviously feeling very guilty about it.

## Acceptance

To accept what had happened demands two things—time and the willingness to recover. You have to learn how much you can take at a time. There is nothing so tiring as strong emotion and the bereaved person is often very tired indeed. You must learn how much you can bear of the company of certain people, well-meaning though they may be. Do not push yourself. Above all, never feel inadequate or defeated when you have to give in for a while.

Some days you feel more able to do things than others, so it is only sensible to press ahead then and not to attempt too much on the bad days. This gradual adjustment to life will enable you to regain your balance and perspective. The numb period at the beginning of mourning gives the needed breathing-space to come to terms with changed circumstances. Realization dawns slowly, different aspects become more clear, the future begins to shape itself.

Look at each new problem squarely and deal with it only when it happens—not before.

Within the family, all the members can help each other. How about giving an award to the one who can make the others laugh, however shakily!

So do not worry about tomorrow;
it will have enough worries of its own.
There is no need to add to the troubles
each day brings.

The Gospel of Matthew

# Is there anybody there?

It is easy to understand why the savage separation which death brings makes some people turn to spiritualism in an effort to make contact with the ones they have lost. Every bereaved person longs to speak to them just once more and to know if they are 'all right'. But, to my mind, this reveals a selfish element in our love. Instead of letting them go, we are trying to bind them to an earthly existence when they have been set free to continue their journey in a new place and time-scale. Instead of allowing them to go forward, we are trying to hold them back. Is it really love or is it self-concern on our part? Are we putting our sorrow before their new opportunities?

For a Christian, this attempt to keep them here on earth, where we know what is going on, shows a lack of trust in a loving God. He is Father of us all and loves us all equally, so we can safely commit our dead into his safe keeping, remembering that he has also promised strength and guidance for those left behind. We need fear neither for them

nor for ourselves. All very fine in theory but no defence against the pangs of mourning we all suffer . . . but, we are not alone—God bears our cross with us. As we pass through this painful experience with him for company, we discover on the other side that the end of the way is joy. And joy is stronger than suffering because beyond the cross is the resurrection.

# Do you want to recover?

When we lose someone we have loved deeply and relied on, life loses most of its purpose. All our emotional energies are directed towards grieving for that person and our own loss. We are knocked sideways, unable to face the world. But sooner or later we have to make a fresh start. The longer the period of mourning has been, the more courage it will take to risk being hurt by life again. Some people take refuge in 'I don't feel very well' or 'no one would want *me*!' Others, having become used to sympathy, forbearance and—dare I say it?—the limelight, find they do not . *want* to rejoin the rat race.

## Turning points

Another obstacle which some people find at the start of their new life is a sense of disloyalty to the dead person. They feel it is wrong when they occasionally experience a pang of joy. They feel ashamed when they find they have forgotten their grief when they are with friends. But this is how it should be. He or she wasn't at the forefront of your mind every minute of every day when alive; neither should he be now. These times of forgetting, happiness even, are

to be welcomed. They show that true healing is well under way.

One woman said she knew the worst was over when she went up to the loft to check that the lagging round the tank was in place before the winter without even thinking that this was a job her husband would have done.

Slowly, the piercing pain of grief will give place to the dull ache of mourning and then to lengthening periods of calm when memories bring more happiness than sorrow. You will know, then, that all is well.

## Take stock

This is the time to take stock. Consider new interests. Get in touch with old friends. Make plans, however restricted they may have to be. Do not make loneliness a way of life—that would be a poor tribute to the person you have lost.

Take stock of yourself, as well. Respect your body and mind when they tell you you have overdone things. If you are tired, have a rest and do the ironing later. If you are holding down a job *and* keeping the family together, don't be too proud to accept any offer of help during the week so that you will have more time to spend with the children at the weekend.

There will still come days when nothing seems worthwhile, or there's no one to do anything for, or you think 'Who cares, anyway?' It helped me to recall the mediaeval philosophy that the smallest thing done well—arranging a vase of flowers, carving a piece of wood, weeding a flower-bed—*anything* which adds to the goodness and beauty of the world satisfies the worker and gives glory to the Creator.

# Mourning

Grief is what we experience after bereavement: mourning is the way in which we express it. Mourning is of the utmost importance because it is the working out of grief. To bottle it up is a great mistake.

# Rituals and conventions

A generation ago, the whole community would be affected by a death. Blinds were drawn in the house of the bereaved family and in the windows of houses along the route taken by the funeral procession. Black crêpe ribbons hung on the doors. When the hearse passed by, people stood still or raised their hats and lowered their eyes. Relatives dressed in black, used black-edged paper for their letters, wore veils in public, stayed indoors for a time and cancelled all social engagements for several months. Society recognized that mourners were people with a special role in the life of the community.

## Security

Much of this seems to us, now, an excessive and morbid attitude to death, but it had its advantages. The mourners, in particular, knew what was expected of them and it gave them security in a world which had tumbled about their ears. They knew the part they had to play and as the prescribed period of mourning slipped away, so, usually, did their own grief. A definite pattern of mourning was comforting to conform to and in most cases it 'worked'. Gradual physical emergence into the world again coincided with gradual emotional emergence as well. The rites and customs had been observed; life could continue.

## The modern taboo

Today, we are less willing to face the fact of death. True, certain rituals are observed, at least in the first few days. We write to the family concerned, send flowers, ask if we can do anything to help. Then we try to dismiss the whole subject from our minds—it strikes too near home and makes us fear for ourselves.

The modern attitude to grief makes it much more difficult to mourn adequately. We have been indoctrinated with the idea that to mourn for longer than a week or two shows a weakness of will, if not sheer self-indulgence. Because death is nowadays a forbidden subject, it is more difficult to impress on those who do not understand that, far from being morbid or thoughtless, mourning is a psychological necessity.

## Going to the funeral

No one enjoys going to a funeral. It is distressing to see the grief of those who mourn, but the sympathy of neighbours and the respect for grief has tremendous value in supporting the bereaved within a comforting framework of convention.

The vast majority of mourners derive much consolation from the service itself. The words seem to stick in their minds and come back to them in the weeks that follow. A widower told the minister after his wife's funeral, 'It said all the things I couldn't say myself.' A widow explained how surprised she had been to see so many in church—'I felt so proud of him . . . all those people . . . they must have thought the world of him.'

## Loose ends

The funeral is the last service (in both senses) that we do for our dead but I believe it is of even greater service to the living. It ties up the loose ends of the life which is over; it reassures us that we have done everything necessary on a practical plane. 'We gave him a good send-off, didn't we?' was how one widow put it. 'It tidies everything up,' said another, 'now I feel I can start again—a bit like Monday morning.'

*This Irish wake (1882) exemplifies a ritual that can give emotional release.*

# Sighing and crying

There's nothing like a good cry. Sighing and crying are the most obvious and most understandable expressions of grief, and doctors agree that if we repress these two outlets, or are denied them by others, we are more likely to become disturbed later on. This is borne out by the man who showed no outward sign of grief after his wife's death but some years later, after visiting his sick sister in the same hospital, suffered a nervous breakdown.

## Natural sorrow

For a while, we have to let ourselves down lightly and not fight to keep up appearances or conform to attitudes demanded by modern society. I remember at the time of the Six Days' War in Israel seeing newspaper photographs of Jewish and Arab women sobbing uncontrollably, their faces crumpled and twisted by the intensity of their grief. Many readers of that paper wrote to the editor complaining that it was wrong for outsiders to see such sorrow. I took the opposite view—I thought, as I looked at those women, 'How right they are to give full expression to their feelings. This is the real work of mourning—they will come through.' And, supported by the sympathy and prayers of people thousands of miles away, I think they did.

## Bad taste

But not everyone is able to let themselves go in this way. Older people, brought up in times when it was considered bad taste to show any strong emotion, will often hold themselves on a very tight rein. I was recently at the funeral of an elderly man; his widow was quietly crying and her sister leaned across and said, loudly, 'Stop it, Elizabeth, everyone's looking at you.' Later, that widow bitterly resented the fact that even more attention had been focused on her and had made it impossible for her to 'take the funeral in'.

---

We don't really want grief, in its first agonies, to be prolonged: nobody could. But we want something else of which grief is a frequent symptom, and then we confuse the symptom with the thing itself. I wrote the other night that bereavement is not the truncation of married love but one of its regular phases—like the honeymoon. What we want is to live our marriage well and faithfully through that phase too. If it hurts (and it certainly will) we accept the pains as a necessary part of this phase. We don't want to escape them at the price of desertion or divorce . . . We will still be married, still in love. Therefore we shall still ache. But we are not at all—if we understand ourselves—seeking the aches for their own sake.

*A Grief Observed*, C. S. Lewis

---

## Barriers

Mourners who suffer most are those who are surrounded by relatives or friends with whom they cannot be natural. Some parents find it impossible to talk about the death with their children; some feel, mistakenly, that the children must be shielded from grief. Some cannot turn to elderly parents for help because they don't want to upset them. Some have quarrelled with their parents or their in-laws and have no point of contact with them any more. Many women, having fought long and hard to establish a reputation for self-sufficiency and competence in a man's world, dare not now 'let themselves down' as they call it or admit that they are *not* invincible or possessed of unassailable self-control.

---

## Manly grief

Men can be particularly hard hit in bereavement because of the traditional 'stiff upper-lip' attitude which most have been taught to assume. Few allow themselves to cry in public. Many feel they cannot do so even within the family and suffer accordingly. But boys, in particular, benefit from seeing their father's tears. Imagine the conflict in a lad who imagines it is unmanly to cry and yet whose most urgent need is to release his desperation in this way. He may well be surprised, even shocked, to see his own father cry, but he will also learn that there is nothing wrong in the natural expression of grief and that tears at such a time have dignity and worth. Father and son can then grieve together and comfort each other.

If you repress every emotion, you create a barrier around yourself which no one can penetrate. It shuts you in and keeps other people out. You condemn yourself to suffer alone—and that is loneliness indeed.

---

## Solidarity

The same expressions of grief which can drive people away from those who mourn can also be a means of drawing together those chiefly concerned. Children should be allowed to join in the tears of bereaved parents. In the early stages, tears come frequently and unexpectedly but soon a pattern of recovery begins to form—the one who stops crying first comforts the others and you all continue with the task in hand.

# What will it mean?

# Who am I?

We all need someone to love who loves us, and when a close relationship is broken we feel painfully alone. A widow who lost her husband, her mother and her sister, all within a year, explained, 'I don't feel special any more. I miss being cherished.' Many married people tend to think alike on most things, so when one of them dies, it is as though half the other dies with them, and therefore half the assurance, half the security.

## Loss of your role

Provided the bereaved family is not suffering actual hardship, the afflictions are mainly psychological. One bewildered woman said, 'You feel as though you were in a train which has gone on and left you in a siding.'

Something we have to guard against is getting *used* to living on the edge of other peoples' lives, reading about and listening to what everyone else is doing but taking no steps to join in.

You have lost your role in life. After the death of a husband, most women find they are now the head of the family, and it stops them in their tracks. Instead of being a husband, a man is now a widower and, however young, somehow pathetic.

## Unnerving

Most marriages exist within a framework of sharing, more so now when wives and husbands both at work arrange between them the jobs to be done. So it is quite unnerving when a widow has to tackle 'his' jobs for the first time. Take the morning post—buff envelopes nearly always spell trouble, demands of some kind, which were previously dealt with by the husband.

In the early days of my widowhood, I felt guilty about opening letters addressed to my husband and some days found myself putting them on one side 'for when he comes home.' Other days, I used to stare at the envelopes and think, 'Who is Mr V. B. Richardson?—he doesn't exist.'

At parties, people often ask 'What does your husband do?' and when I say that he's dead they rarely ask 'What do *you* do?' How do they think widows live these days without doing *something*, I wonder! So a widow often asks herself 'Who am I?'

## Life without a partner

On the domestic front, it is undoubtedly harder to be a widower than a widow. Elderly men cannot imagine the rest of their lives without the one with whom they had shared everything. And younger men often feel inadequate when faced with running a home and bringing up children. However, a man does have his job, which helps him take his mind off things while he is at work. It is also much easier for a man to re-marry, however many children he has.

## Widows

The problems facing widows are also highly alarming. Among them are bewilderment, fear of breakdown, of financial difficulties, and of being pushed into the background by people generally.

The modern family has become much more self-contained than the old extended family all living within easy reach. Husbands and wives have come

to rely only on each other, and even when the wife has a job of her own, his death will seriously cut back what she does.

It takes time to learn to speak in the singular instead of the plural. You still hear yourself saying, 'Borrow *our* car' or 'Come round to *our* house.' In the case of wives who have become almost dependent on 'what my husband says', fear may assume panic proportions. However, there are people to give advice and organizations that help.

### Some helpful organizations

CRUSE uses local contacts to advise widows. (126 Sheen Road, Richmond, Surrey, TW9 1UR. 01-948 4818.)
SAMARITANS runs a 24-hour telephone service for all in despair or trouble. (Local address in your telephone directory.)
NATIONAL COUNCIL FOR THE SINGLE WOMAN AND HER DEPENDENTS provides welfare safeguards. (29 Chilworth Mews, London, W2. 01-262 1451.)

## Second adolescence

It is surprising how like a teenager you feel as a result of bereavement. There are the same unpredictable moods, the same periods of lethargy followed by bouts of over-activity, the same enthusiasms which fizzle out, the same hopes drowned in the same despairs. Other bereaved people have told me that they felt humiliated by such juvenile emotions and fought them violently.

In the same way that an adolescent isn't always sure where he fits in, the bereaved person finds it difficult to decide into which age-group he or she falls. This is especially true of the middle-aged. You haven't the same footing as grandparents; yet you are out of touch with young parents. You have little in common with single people whose lifestyle has been quite different.

In addition, a widow often feels that being 'just a housewife' is no longer satisfying.

# Who do they think I am?

I once read an article by a young widow who said, 'Being reduced to single living again is a horrible state—other people look on you as an emotional cripple and a second-class person.'

## Humiliations

When a woman loses her husband (and, to a lesser degree, when a man loses his wife) other people are as confused by her change of status as she is. Western society inflicts many humiliations on single people. A widow is only half a pair—she makes an uneven number at a table; she tends to stick out like a sore thumb and, worse still, is a constant reminder that any of those with her may be in her position one day. Men are more fortunate, here, as there is a shortage of single men and a man can more easily find someone to take out with him.

It is essential to cultivate a sense of humour in order to survive the slights and thoughtless suggestions which will come your way. A friend told me, 'Acquaintances will cross the road rather than speak to you—it's as though they'd seen a Martian with antennae and green scales.' Another widow described how she swung between laughter and tears when people met her in the street and asked 'Are you feeling better, now?' as though she'd had a nasty attack of flu.

## Neglected or suspected

Fears that you may be forgotten or

written off are not without foundation. A widow tends to be asked round for a cup of tea rather than to supper. You feel you are now deemed fit only for female company: there is a widespread suspicion that all widows are husband-hunting. The sudden loss of masculine company is a deprivation for widows of all ages.

At a time when nerve-endings are raw and exposed, it isn't easy to be brave and make yourself vulnerable to heart-ache. Like it or not, however, it is essential to fight your way back into your circle of friends. But we must make allowances for those who cannot possibly understand what bereavement means . . . yet. We must learn to laugh at the ridiculous side of many situations in which we find ourselves.

## A new start

Any form of deep suffering makes or breaks us. The experience of millions who have been through it is that when we feel most broken, that is the point from which we can start again. Every bereaved person is diminished, but faith can build us up once more. A widow told me, 'I can only keep going by reminding myself that I still matter to God and that I'm still important to him.'

# Regaining strength

The chief emotion of anyone meeting a bereaved person for the first time is one of acute embarrassment. They don't want to upset you and they don't know what to say. Above all, they dread a public display of tears. In the past, many of us will have felt the same so we can understand their wariness.

## Making the first move

We learn that, hard though it is, it is up to *us* to make the first move. *We* have to be the ones to go up to an acquaintance in the supermarket and say hello. Once the ice has been broken, we no longer find ourselves playing hide and seek among the baked beans and we can talk more normally. News will get round that you have neither been struck dumb nor made mentally deficient—two conditions often absurdly associated with bereavement! Some people will be over-bracing and treat you as they would a child recovering from mumps. Some will speak in hushed voices and urge you to rest. But everyone means well and is doing their best—our part is to be grateful and to help them out.

Starting again is an exhausting business. Now, it's *you* who have to make all the running to keep in touch with people. In a world geared to couples, it becomes a battle to see yourself as a person in your own right, and to persuade others to do so.

## Join in

Gradually, you will receive invitations again. However little you feel like accepting them, make the effort because, otherwise, people's embarrassment will soon turn to boredom and you may not be asked again. Go along, smile and join in.

Little by little, enjoyment will replace the anguish of going alone and when you actually ask someone to come for a meal, you will know that another hurdle is over and you are beginning to find your feet again. It will take courage to return alone to an empty house or sleeping children, and no one to talk over the evening with. But we have to make the choice—either to face the world on its own terms or become a forgotten recluse.

## A simple meal

I have heard many widows explain that they can no longer have friends round now that there is no man to take his share in the conversation. I suspect that is an excuse rather than a reason! As a first step, why not ask someone who has been a particular help to you to come and share your main meal? You need not put on anything special. Children love to help in the preparations and to be allowed to take part, at least for the first half-hour, and benefit from being considered adult enough to do so.

Try to do things a little differently from when you entertained as a couple —it will help you to begin your new way of life. Go and browse round the bookshops and you will be sure to find an interesting recipe book. Try a new dish you have not made before. There are plenty of simple cookery books available which show you how to make a tasty, attractive meal.

## Courage to continue

Supporting hands abound for the first few months, but you can't expect to be carried on other people's shoulders for ever. The temptation then is to let yourself go. Not to bother with cooking yourself a meal, not to care how you look, taking less interest in things outside your own small world. The fight is on against self-centredness. You have to make another effort—but the self-discipline involved in taking a pride in yourself, even with no one else to notice, brings its own reward of self-respect and confidence.

Christians do not have a monopoly of courage and inner resources. Trust in the goodness of God and in his guiding hand on life obviously provides a security, but there are countless men and women who face bereavement, adjust to it, cope with it and make something good and worthwhile out of it with little or no spiritual support.

## Bad patches

From time to time, something happens or is said, usually out of the blue, which re-opens the old wounds and tears us apart again. One widow told of a morning when the sun was shining, the children were doing well at school and she herself felt that day able to cope with anything. She turned on the radio and heard a voice describing the place where she and her husband had spent their honeymoon. Desolation overcame her and she sat and wept.

Months—even years—later, such dark times come and remind us how fragile is our resilience. If we need help, it is only sensible to ask for it. Don't be ashamed of yourself—admit how you feel. An understanding friend or a good neighbour will usually be available to encourage you until the cloud lifts.

## A new viewpoint

Christians often feel guilty when they are depressed. We feel that because faith upheld us at the time of acute crisis, it will automatically go on doing so. But times change and *we* change; we begin to ask questions which did not occur to us then; faith may waver. This is when we need to be humble enough to recognize our need of someone else's opinion or assurance and to go to someone we can trust to help us. It is possible to rely too much on our own resources of prayer and our own reading of the Bible. It is tempting to read what we want to believe into a section of the Bible or to pray too self-centredly. Then, a different view may be all we need to set us on our way again. *Our* faith may have wavered, but God remains faithful.

# Keeping well

A doctor once said that bereavement was like having a surgical operation without an anaesthetic. You will feel very tired, but this is not to say that you must sit down and rest all day. By all means rest whenever you feel a real need to do so, but remember that exercise is also necessary.

A brisk walk each day will give you fresh air and the chance to meet other people for a casual chat. Physical exercise will make you healthily tired so that you sleep better, and will also keep your muscles in trim. Fear and anxiety cause adrenalin to be pumped into the system, making muscles tense. Adrenalin supplies the energy for bodily activity, so if we don't use our muscles or take enough exercise, it does not get used up. This sets up more tension and frustration.

## A broken heart

Some people fear they will die of a 'broken heart'. This image arises from ancient beliefs that the heart was the chief seat of the emotions. Such expressions are often found in the Old Testament. But we must not take this idea literally. Occasionally, the surviving partner of a marriage may suffer some form of heart disease, but it has not been proved that grief alone is the cause. There are nearly always contributory factors. Understandable though it may be for the distressed person to turn to alcohol, tobacco or pills to dull the ache, the dangers are well-known and a growing dependence on any of them will do harm.

## A proper diet

Strong emotion often takes away the desire for food. It is common for the

*A healthy diet should include every day something from each of the types of food shown above. Proteins, fats and carbohydrates supply the energy we need.*

bereaved person to feel 'full up', even nauseated at the thought of food. Some, even though they feel hungry, will make do with insufficient food because the effort to cook a meal is too great.

But, however little you feel like cooking or eating, it is essential (as when recovering from illness) to get your strength back and live sensibly. It is foolish to risk being a worry to other people or becoming dependent on them to do something you *can* do for yourself. Large meals are not called for; it is better to have nutritious foods, little and often.

## 'I can't sleep'

Most bereaved people say how they dread sleepless nights of tossing and turning, reliving the past and worrying about the future. Commonly the pattern of sleep is so disturbed that the morning brings a headache as bad as the heartache. Many fear that if they don't get enough sleep they will be ill. This is not true; given the right conditions—a comfortable bed, warmth, relaxation and tiredness—sleep will eventually come. Don't *worry* about not sleeping— that is enough on its own to keep sleep away.

Fortunately, there are several things you can do. First, see your doctor. If he thinks it necessary, he will prescribe a short course of sleeping-pills to break the pattern of sleepless nights. Then being active during the day will encourage natural sleep. A warm bath followed by a warm drink helps you to relax. If there is now no one to bring you a drink in bed, take a small vacuum flask of boiling water with you so that you can easily make yourself a drink. Have a tin of biscuits by the bed—you won't sleep if you're hungry.

Make sure you are warm. Bed is a

Ways to help relax

Deep, calm breathing

Leisurely walk

Shoulder shrugs

Soothing music

Rolling head slowly

Warm bath

Light book

cold place when you have been used to another's warmth, and an electric blanket is well worth having.

## Reading and listening

If you like reading in bed, you may find an undemanding book or magazine will divert the mind from its whirl of thoughts. Television is another possibility. So is a transistor radio! I am not suggesting that everyone tunes into loud pop music or stimulating phone-in programmes—these would probably send sleep fleeing for some. Those who enjoy news bulletins, documentaries, musical concerts and so on, may find the BBC World Service, transmitted right through the night, well worth listening to. The sound of a friendly, and quickly familiar, voice can be a comfort, and it may soothe you to sleep.

When all else fails, remind yourself that not being able to sleep is not medically harmful. So lie quietly and relaxed; put away the worries of yesterday and anxiety about tomorrow. And take advantage of the uninterrupted quiet. There is time to remember the good things and be thankful for what remains. A sleepless night can be the opportunity to commit yourself into God's loving hands, *expecting* the peace he has promised to all who ask for it. The strength to do what we have to comes only when it is needed—not before. God's help is always given at the right time.

## Psychological helps

When you are low it seems impossible to 'think happy'. Yet attitudes of mind *do* influence bodily well-being, so it is a good idea to expect something *good* to happen each day. From there you may be able to plan to make it happen. This is one way towards returning self-confidence.

Self-respect may be at a low ebb, too, so it is important to keep up your past standards. Tempting though it may be to slop around the house untidily, it pays to make an effort and dress properly. To see you looking good will make those around you feel that you consider them worth making this effort for Widowers, too, benefit from keeping a smart appearance, even if it now means using a launderette and doing the ironing. Something new to wear, or a record, book or toy, can cheer up a bereaved child.

# How the church can help

Don't hesitate about going to church at a time of crisis—even if you have never been before. Ignore the mutterings of bad neighbours. To be welcoming is one of the functions of the church—to be a refuge for those who suffer, and to help *any* who feel the need to find out what God has to say to them at this low point in their life.

## A fuller life

Many find their loneliness lessened by joining a church group. They find that churches are, by and large, friendly and ready to help. Nearly all churches have neighbourhood schemes by which they come to hear of people in special need. By taking advantage of what the church offers socially, widows and widowers and their families can be drawn into activities which they will enjoy and look forward to. Some may find they want to attend a service and, against all expectation, discover the beginning of a fuller life, spiritually as well as socially.

Every town and village will have a church and no one need hesitate to take a step in its direction.

## In your own time

One of the hardest things for some bereaved Christians is to get back into the life of the church. When the whole family once sat, Sunday by Sunday, taking part in the familiar service, going to church may be hard to bear.

As always, the sooner we can pick up the threads the easier it will be, but if the bereaved family feels unable to join in Sunday worship for a time, they should not feel guilty about it. The church shouldn't expect too much too soon. The church members can show the warmth of their caring in practical ways, giving sympathy and loving comfort, assuring the family of their prayers on their behalf—and no one who has not experienced this can appreciate fully the strength God gives in answer to other people's prayers.

# Emotional problems

# Loneliness

After the death of a husband or wife, we gradually turn to others for company. This is right—what is self-defeating is if we become so dependent on having people with us that we can't bear being alone. We all need some solitude in order to sort ourselves out. It will largely be up to us to arrange our lives so that these times of being alone are balanced by time spent with other people.

## Reminders

Just as the setting up of a 'shrine' to the dead person only makes the pain last longer, so it is only common sense to avoid the things you know are likely to upset you—an old photograph, a place which had a special meaning for you both. Some people, though, are comforted by photographs: one man I know had framed every picture of his wife he could find. But another friend put away everything which would remind her of her dead son. In time, as her anguish lessened, she put up one or two photographs and found they did help her. Do whatever helps *you*, always realizing that life has to go on and that the past mustn't smother the future.

## Our own life

It becomes all too easy to live life through other people—watching television, reading the paper. It is *our* life we have to live. If we want friends who will relieve our loneliness, we have to be friendly ourselves; to benefit from others' efforts we have to make an effort ourselves. It is tiring but it is the worthwhile price to pay for getting back into the world. The worst thing the lonely person can do is to sit at home and feel sorry for himself. If you can, go out at least once a day and if possible at about the same time. People are creatures of habit—it will be easier to smile at someone you meet regularly, and soon you will be on speaking terms.

## A wider horizon

It is surprising but true that there seems no need for anyone to be physically lonely. Everywhere there are clubs and organizations for the lonely. Joining a group of people with similar interests will do the whole family good. The bereaved person can become bogged down with child-minding and keeping the home together, so it is important that the horizons should be widened. For many people these clubs have provided just what they needed: practical help and moral support.

At the same time, they recognize the dangers of catering for only one type of person, the danger of serving more to emphasize the loneliness and separation than to lessen it. And so they all aim at enabling their members gradually to wean themselves away as they feel able. Information about clubs and organizations can be found in your local library, newspaper or information bureau.

# Sharing your home

If the prospect of living alone is unbearable, you may consider setting up house with a friend or relative. This arrangement can be highly successful or quite disastrous. The saying, 'You never really know a person until you live with them', is very true. Ensure that you will be able to get on together before committing yourself. Take time to talk about your interests, families, likes and dislikes. Bear in mind that you may both find it difficult to adapt.

When you have decided on a person you think suitable, it may help if you agree that the first fortnight will be a trial period, if circumstances make this possible. At the end of that time you'll know how you get along together.

## Fair deal

A shared home usually means that one of you will have to give up most of his own furniture and goods, and may

### Money matters
Fix fair rent for area; agree method of splitting gas, electricity and phone bills and household expenses.

always feel hard done by. Discuss this honestly beforehand.

Certain questions will have to be asked. How are the financial arrangements to work? Will you live separate lives or do most things together? Having decided what you want, can you see the other person being willing to co-operate on those terms? How far are *you* willing to give way?

When you are thinking of any kind of sharing, it is wise to have a proper agreement drawn up so that each person knows exactly what is expected. This sounds cold-blooded, but it will save much argument if difficulties should arise later on.

# Sexual deprivation

An aspect of bereavement not often enough acknowledged is sexual deprivation. Whatever one may sometimes be told, it is impossible completely to direct one's sexuality into other channels. Death snatches away the deepest human expression of love, leaving an emptiness which nothing else can fill. The sudden cutting off of the sex life of a widow or widower sets up deep tensions. What to do with one's sex drive is a very real problem.

Sexual deprivation adds to loneliness. One widow said that what she missed most after her husband's death was being touched. Bed is a cold place for the bereaved wife or husband. It is not only the sexual acts themselves which are missed, it's the little things—a caress in passing, the joke which no one else sees. To see other people enjoying these can be a painful reminder that you have lost part of yourself.

## Casual relationships

Men and women need each other; we all need to hold and be held. Yet to take up some uncommitted sexual relationship is not the answer. Without the depth and commitment of marriage, such an affair is always second-best. The longing to love and be loved is in no way wrong in itself. But in this situation, as Cardinal Basil Hume has written, 'It is not right to allow other people to fall in love with us . . . if we are silly (and vanity can be the danger here) we may cause pain and hurt, and that is wrong.' For some, masturbation may bring temporary physical release, but the basic need to give oneself to another will not be met and the deprivation may even be intensified.

## Responsible involvement

This is an area where the Christian is hard hit. Magazines and television all insist that frequent sex is necessary for all, and no concern of anyone except the individuals involved. But Christians believe that the act of sex is the total involvement of one person with another, a complete self-giving. Sex is never an isolated act. There are social as well as personal implications to be considered. Sexual satisfaction is not to be an irresponsible indulgence. We believe that sex is a gift from God to be enjoyed but not selfishly exploited.

To be deprived of one's sex-life need not be fatal! At the time, when I was quite sure it would be, I read some perceptive words by a young American widow—'While the human organism can get along without physical love-making, it cannot thrive without human affection.' What the bereaved need most is warm concern and continuing love and tenderness.

# Re-marriage

At the time of bereavement the idea of marrying again will be unthinkable, but people *do* re-marry—a high proportion of widowers do so within five years of losing their wives. A second marriage should be seen as a compliment to the previous partner: never think of it as in any way disloyal. Every relationship is unique. No one need condemn himself to a bleak lifetime of living on past memories and loyalties. Even so, many *do* feel a sense of betrayal when contemplating a second marriage. Before entering into a new relationship it is essential to say goodbye to the old one—not forgetting it, but letting it go, never allowing it to come between you and your new life.

A second marriage calls for courage, commitment and a degree of tolerance which can be demanding. But, given the essential ingredients of love and understanding, making it work can bring a deep sense of achievement and fulfilment.

## Realistic expectations

Bereavement weakens one's self-confidence and the longing for support is sometimes overwhelming, especially when there are young children to bring up alone. The prospect of someone to share the responsibility can be very attractive. For a man, the thought of supporting a new wife and step-children, as well as any children he may have himself, can be daunting. But, delicate though the situation may be, the adjustments need not be too much to cope with. Much of the tension which may arise early in a second marriage comes from fear that you may not live up to the ideals of your new spouse. But

you are both as you are—there is no need to compare the new relationship with the old. It should be seen as a new beginning in both your lives. If a first marriage was happy, a second is likely to be so, too. Past experience will have shown allowances have to be made all round, and any wisdom you gained from your first partnership can be brought to bear on the second.

## Stepchildren

By the time of your second marriage, the children will already be getting to know their new step-parent quite well, and they will be happy for you. But if they are younger they may guard your love for them jealously, not wanting to have to share you with someone else. In this situation, you will need to show them that you still love them just as much.

A useful book on remarriage and children is Brenda Maddox, *Living with other people's children*, Deutsch.

If your new partner also has children, it may help, if you can afford it, to start afresh in a new home. This avoids the problem of children resenting the intrusion of others into what has been their territory until now. In any case, you are going to have to encourage a great deal of giving and sharing.

Discipline is a tricky subject, and you may find that your new partner has different views from your own. You are both now responsible for both sets of children, so it is important to follow an agreed, consistent course.

# Where to live – and how

All sorts of practical problems arise almost at once when you have lost your husband or wife. Fortunately, most questions can be left for a while until you are better able to deal with them.

## Decisions, decisions

Don't do anything in a hurry. If it is at all possible major decisions should be postponed for at least six months. At first, judgement is unlikely to be reliable and it will be difficult to see things clearly. A line of action which seems best at the time may prove a mistake.

Never be afraid to ask for advice and opinion on those matters which you don't know about. Most people are more than willing to make suggestions. Not all of these will be equally helpful, but accept them in the spirit in which they are given, weigh up all the arguments and keep them in your mind until you feel able to come to a sensible decision. Business friends or workmates will be able to help in their own fields, neighbours will come and help in the house, and your priest or minister will want to share with you Christian comfort and strength.

# How shall we manage?

Nearly all bereaved families find themselves worse off financially, so the first problem to solve is how to manage with the money available. This is true even when it is the wife who has died,

because the husband may have to arrange for any children to be looked after. If they are very young, he may have to give up his job, at least temporarily, in order to care for them.

This will mean living on whatever savings he has, plus any social-security and family-allowance benefits he may be entitled to. If there are no relatives or friends who can take the children in, they may have to be put in the care of the local authority, or the father may have to arrange for paid help in the home, which can be very expensive indeed. See also pages 56–57.

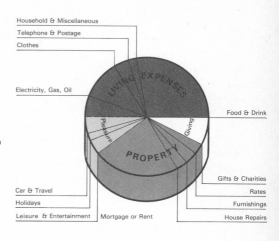

Household & Miscellaneous
Telephone & Postage
Clothes
Electricity, Gas, Oil
LIVING EXPENSES
Pleasure
Giving
PROPERTY
Food & Drink
Gifts & Charities
Rates
Furnishings
Car & Travel
Holidays
Leisure & Entertainment
Mortgage or Rent
House Repairs

## A basic year's budget

As soon as you know how much money will be available for living expenses, it helps to draw up a simple budget, at least for the first year. A widow will probably need to supplement her pension and allowances, especially if she has children to support. She may know already how much she needs to cover food, clothing, school expenses and so on but may have little knowledge of how much she will need for rent and rates, heating, telephone, licences, insurance and all the big bills which come when she is least prepared to deal with them. These can add up to an alarming amount, and a detailed list of what they are and when they fall due will make it easier to see where cut-backs have to be made. Once your financial position is clear, it is worth asking the social-security department whether you are eligible for any extra allowances.

## Making economies

Although it is important not to cut back on items like proper food, it is often easy to make substantial savings, particularly by re-organizing your largest expenses. If you run a car, you may decide that you could make do with public transport. You may be able to take holidays out of peak season. It may be possible to save by adjusting heaters so that rooms are kept at a lower temperature when not in use. Proper insulation in the loft and lagging of the hot-water tank will also cut fuel costs fast. Double glazing is not as effective at reducing heat loss.

# Where shall we live?

A common reaction to bereavement is the feeling that you must move right away to a new area where no one knows you and you can start again. More common still is the desire to move house in order to be near a relative, friend or married child.

## A careful decision

But this decision should not be taken without a great deal of thought. Over and over again, one hears of a hurried move to a strange part of the country where the bereaved person no longer has the comfort of familiar landmarks and finds that few people are interested in his/her troubles.

One elderly widower could not bear to go on living in the old home after his wife died, so against all advice he sold up and bought a house in the same town as his married daughter. Soon after, his son-in-law was sent abroad for two years and the old man had no one of his own to visit or talk to. He became more and more of a recluse, and before the two years were up, he too had died.

There are now several thousand housing associations—independent organizations which aim to provide good rented accommodation—around the country. Find out about schemes in your area from the Citizens' Advice Bureau, or The National Federation of Housing Associations, 30-32 Southampton Street, London, WC2.

Of course, it can be a *good* idea to move. The important thing to remember is that this step should only be taken when you are sure you are no longer dependent on your present neighbours and environment. For parents, the decision to move will probably be made when the last child leaves home. For others the decision may come when friends retire and move away. By then, you will be able to see more clearly what you want to do and where you want to be.

Few widows have any choice but to give up their homes; lack of money forces it on them and they have to look around for a smaller house which will be cheaper to run. Some will be able to stay where they are, however, either because their husband's life insurance was linked to the mortgage or because they have a sufficient income.

## Restlessness

Acute restlessness is common in bereavement. This may take the form of frequent visits to people around the country. Friends and relatives will not like to say 'No' when you invite yourself for a day or two, but hectic travel is best avoided or at least postponed. Other people are usually leading busy lives and your self-absorption and possibly somewhat irrational behaviour will not make you a wholly welcome guest.

The wife of someone I knew was widowed while she and her husband were on holiday. The chain of events following her bereavement presents a classic example of bad advice. She sold the house from a distance because she could not bear the thought of coming back; she moved round the country from married child to married child; she stayed two or three nights with various friends in turn, living out of her suitcase for months on end. She never came to terms with what had happened, was bereft of old friends in her own neighbourhood, at the mercy of estate agents and quack medical opinions, and prey to every fear that a vivid imagination could produce. In the end she bought a cottage in a remote Northumberland village where she and her husband had once spent a holiday.

You can't run away from your situation. Wherever you go, your grief goes with you. Until you have worked through it, you are better in your own place, among your own people.

## Staying where you are

In the same way, it isn't always a good idea to accept kindly-meant offers of hospitality immediately after bereavement. Going away is always easier than coming back. If you feel you must have extra support—either because there will be no one else in the house or because there are young children to cope with—accept an offer from someone sympathetic to come and stay with you for a short time. That way, you will not sit about with nothing to do but think, you will not have to be a 'good guest', and you will be able to do the day-to-day jobs as usual.

Sometimes, to be in someone else's house with little to do and worrying about what needs to be done at home adds to the alarm and frustration. It is better to stick it out and begin to come to terms with the situation, and then, when you feel reasonably confident of being able to return home without too much pain, to spend a short time away with friendly and agreeable people.

By that time, you will be needing a rest and will be able to relax better for knowing that the immediate decisions have been taken and jobs attended to. Being away from it all will then provide a sense of balance and proportion to enable you to look ahead sensibly. When you do go back, it helps immeasurably to have someone with you to stay just long enough to see you settled in.

## If you have to move

It is doubly hard that the problems of finding a new home come at a time when you are least able to cope with it all. A widow finds herself at a disadvantage because it is sometimes more difficult for her to obtain a mortgage. If a widow with children decides to try for rented accommodation, she may find private landlords unwilling to let to a single-parent family, especially if the children are very young. And there may be a long waiting-list for council property. Even if she has been renting from a local authority, she may find the tenancy is not transferable. If she moves away from the district and applies to the new authority, she will of course go to the bottom of the list and have to find temporary accommodation.

If you find it difficult to pay your rent you may be able to claim a rent rebate. The amount depends on your total income, your rent, and your family circumstances. Apply at the rent rebates section at your local council offices. *There's money off rent*, from your local council offices or Citizens' Advice Bureau, gives further information.

## Living with relatives

However tempted and pressurized you may be, consider carefully before agreeing to live with relatives. The practical objection to this is that once you *have* found a roof over your head, the local authority may well assume that there is no hurry to rehouse you and may even move your name lower down the list. The psychological objection is that, understanding and adaptable though your relatives may be, every family needs somewhere of their own where they can work out their problems and attitudes together, free from criticism and unwanted advice.

# Earning a living

# Pros and cons

After where to live, the most pressing problem will be how to make enough money to live on. This will be particularly hard for the young widow with children and also for the young widower who may have to pay for someone to look after the children. The young mother will have to decide whether or not to go out to work. In many cases, she will *have* to. All the same, there are pros and cons to be considered.

Getting a job may not be worth it financially. You will need to work out whether the money you earn will reduce the benefits to which you are entitled. Find out if money will be stopped if you are off sick. Will your going out to work mean that your children will have to be looked after? What will you do in school holidays?

## Finding a job

Even if you decide that you would be better off working, and look for a full-time job outside the home, it may be hard to find one.

You need to ask yourself: 'What do I enjoy doing? What am I *able* to do? What is the effect likely to be on the children? Will it be better to get a job outside the home and have more money, or to stay at home and manage with less? Should I take an outside job so as to help myself, psychologically, and be a more interesting person?'

This can be the time to re-assess your personality; it can be an opportunity to receive that peace of mind which is so necessary. To commit the situation to God and to wait patiently for opportunities is the way to a calm mind.

# Make your house work

If you own your house but may have difficulty in keeping it going, how can the house itself help? Have you, or can your improvise, a spare room? If so, would you be willing to let it? Universities and polytechnics are always desperate to find accommodation for both staff and students.

## Finding a lodger

The advantage of letting a room to someone connected with education is that you will probably have the holidays free, while still receiving a small retaining fee. Decide whether you would prefer to give someone full board (more of a tie), bed, breakfast and evening meal, bed and breakfast, or accommodation only. Find out whether your lodger will be there at weekends and if so whether the same meals arrangement will apply. Discuss with them whether they wish to share everything with you and your family, or whether they are to live on a bed-sit basis, with shared bathroom, cooking in their room.

Decide whether you want a man, woman, boy or girl. What sort of age would you prefer—a young student, a slightly older person, a middle-aged person perhaps on a temporary assignment in your area? Another adult or near-adult in the house has definite advantages: it means that someone else will be there in case of household disasters or sudden illness; they can also provide new ideas, a more balanced view of life. The mere fact of someone coming in and out may give that extra sense of security you need. A lodger with whom you get on well can be a help in many ways.

## The legal side

A solicitor will advise you on drawing up a properly worded tenancy agreement to protect you from undesirable tenants. Once your tenant has signed the tenancy agreement, you are bound by law to give him a rent book (these can be bought from most stationers). Every time you receive the rent, your tenant should produce the book and you sign it as a receipt.

If you live in rented accommodation, and want to sub-let a room, you will need to ask your landlord for written permission. (A local authority, unfortunately, often puts your rent up when you let a room.) If you have a mortgage you will likewise need to obtain permission to let from your building society.

When you make your tax return you must include any rent you have received. You can, however, deduct the cost of such expenses as preparing the room, putting right any damage caused, and necessary replacement of furnishings.

## Your garden

There are several ways in which even a small garden can bring in a little much-needed money. You could try growing herbs, which take up little room and are much in demand from people wanting to use fresh products rather than dried. Have you fruit-trees or bushes? Can you grow tomatoes? Do you have success with a certain type of flower? If space is limited, it is better to concentrate on one product in order to start to build up a local reputation for it, both privately and among the shops.

---

# Working outside the home

## Using a previous career

What did you do before you married? Was it something you could take up again without too much effort? Were you, perhaps, a typist, a hairdresser, a schoolteacher or a nurse? Whatever you did for a living, even if you haven't kept your hand in, it is possible to take it up again. There is probably an evening class you could attend for a short session until you are competent once more. You may then be able to persuade someone to employ you on trial.

## Giving a service

Are you good at flower-arranging? If so, let people know that you are willing to do the floral decorations for local functions or weddings. An easy way to get your name known is to do your first piece of work for a friend or someone you know in the neighbourhood. If it goes well and complimentary comments are made, not only will your confidence be increased, the orders will soon start coming in. Do you enjoy meeting people and feel you could go round selling cosmetics or other goods to people in their homes? There are often advertisements in the local papers for representatives. The best plan is, first find out what is needed in your own district and then set out to satisfy that need.

## Can you drive?

If you have a car it may now prove too expensive to run and maintain, but a car spells freedom and independence. If you work out the cost of fares on public

**work available outside home**
market research and interviewing
teaching—school/evening class
office work
nursing auxiliary
domestic help
catering—in canteen/for parties
shop assistant
local factory work
gardening
taxi service/driving
decorating/plumbing/odd-jobbing
escorting disabled people

transport for your family, the cost difference may not turn out to be so great. Make enquiries locally and find out if a shop or a firm would employ you as a driver, perhaps part-time. Would it be possible to run a private taxi-service? To do this you will, of course, have to fulfil all the legal requirements and be comprehensively covered by your insurance company.

If you plan to run a small business from your home, you will have to consult the local byelaws as you may need planning permission. If you are in rented accommodation, you will also need the consent of the landlord. If you decide to become a child-minder, you must be registered with the local authority.

Before setting up in business it is worth getting advice from:
the Citizens' Advice Bureau
your bank manager
a solicitor
an accountant
your local Small Firms Information Centre (see telephone directory)

# Earning at home

For a parent with still-young children, this is the ideal way of supplementing the family income. It allows flexibility and does not entail the expenses involved in travelling, dressing well, buying food out, and so on.

## Home cooking

Are you a good cook? Home cooking is always in demand. Again, it would probably be better to concentrate on one thing you know you do well. Your speciality will soon become known and sought after, be it your pastry or your steak-and-kidney pudding. I know one widow who advertised the fact that she would cook as many quiches as people would order. In three months, she had to buy a freezer, to be able to cook in advance for parties and regular orders. In five years she had a chain of shops in four different towns, all turning out her own recipe and expanding all the time.

You may not want to do anything on such a scale, but your own local shops may well be interested.

Start by telling a few people what you intend to do; put an advertisement in your local paper. If you feel able to try your hand at private catering, let it be known that you will suggest menus, cater for, cook and deliver food for small parties.

### Work at home
typing
child-minding
factory outwork e.g. coil winding
embroidery
dressmaking and alterations
carpentry or carving
telephone selling

## Safeguards

Any work done at home is open to exploitation from unscrupulous firms. Setting up a business from home may be quite involved and legal advice should always be obtained before starting. A recent survey shows that many home-workers earn a pittance; the government is on to this, however. Before you decide what you would like to do at home, find out the proper rate for the job in your area.

## Clothing

Other skills much in demand are home dressmaking, crochet and embroidery. If you are good at sewing, you can also earn money by altering clothes, especially children's which are outgrown but not outworn and which need adjustment for the next child.

# The bereaved child

Sooner or later, a child comes home with the news that a friend's Mummy or Daddy has died. Our immediate reaction is to say 'How dreadful!' — and change the subject. But the child may be frightened and bewildered, hit by the fact that death happens not only on TV but to real people and therefore, perhaps, even his own parents.

## Talking about death

This is when we should stop whatever we are doing, express our own shock and sorrow and speak naturally about what has happened. Ask if your child thinks there is anything you could do to help. Suggest that he is particularly kind to his friend — he might ask him or her round to play, for example.

This way of dealing with a terrifying situation will do much to reassure the child. It will give him a chance to help his friend practically. It will also give him a sense of security to know that if it ever happened to him, he would be looked after, and that even such a disaster as this can be coped with.

# When death comes

We must never shut children out of a grief the *whole* family shares. It is impossible completely to protect them from what has happened, but they need not suffer permanent emotional damage. The most unobtrusive way of teaching children how to cope with death is by helping them to see that from time to time suffering comes into every life, as when the cat brings in a bird it has killed. They will experience it in the death of a dearly-loved pet, or even when a friend moves away. It is at such times that we can reassure the child that he is not alone in his sadness and that within the family sorrow is natural.

## Never tell lies

One child was told her Daddy had gone abroad, another that her Mummy was in hospital. Both children eventually heard that their parents had died, and suffered much greater shock, made worse by the permanent distrust they came to feel for all adults and the fear that any separation might mean death.

Honesty is just as essential within a Christian family. The child who said bitterly that God was 'no good' was reacting perfectly rationally to his father's death in a plane crash, for his mother had often said that God would keep him safe. Children soon learn that Christians are not immune to disaster. Always assure them that, for those whose lives are committed to God, *whatever* happens can be turned to good, and that such experiences should give us greater sympathy for all who suffer.

## Some common fears

As well as the shock of unbelief at the death of a parent, a child may be afraid of losing the other as well. He may ask constantly, 'How old are you?' Young children may even think that everyone else in the family is about to die.

Imaginative children may be frightened that the parent's ghost will return and haunt them. Bedtime is dreaded and brings on symptoms such as sweating, bed-wetting and nightmares. Some children insist on having the window closed 'in case Daddy comes in'.

Younger children may worry that Mummy or Daddy will marry someone else, especially if they have read old-fashioned stories about wicked stepmothers. In such cases, a widowed mother must assure them that the man who drops in to do a household job is simply giving a helping hand, while a father can explain that the woman who brings round a cake is being friendly.

It is important to allow the child to talk about his fears so that the hidden ones can be brought into the open and dealt with. If the children withdraw into themselves, we have to watch their reactions carefully. We must be sensitive to try to understand what may be making them anxious.

## A constructive attitude

A child's attitude to death will be coloured by our own. If we have taught our children compassion for others, they will find it easier to accept bereavement. They will tend to assume that as we have previously helped friends, it is now the turn of those friends to do the same for us! This attitude will help prevent bitterness. But we must never deny what has happened. Refusal to face facts will only raise false hopes, confuse the child and make it more difficult for him to adjust.

## Fear, guilt and shock

The effects of bereavement on a child will depend on many things—his age, his own personality and the reactions of the family. When a parent dies, the child feels let down and abandoned. Was it because he was 'naughty' or disobedient? Guilt and self-doubt build up. He remembers the time he said, 'I wish you were dead', and may believe he has actually killed Mummy or Daddy.

Another child may appear to be indifferent or downright callous. Susan was told that her mother had been killed in a car smash. 'Has she?', she said, 'Is tea ready?' This reaction is due to intense shock and is the child's automatic defence mechanism.

# Explaining death

How much to tell a child about death should always depend on how much he wants to know. This will be discovered by the sort of questions he asks. Children soon realize that death marks the end of life (though, as Christians believe, the beginning of another) and that death brings sorrow and grief. But children are as resilient as they are vulnerable, and with help and support they can survive almost any experience so long as they are surrounded by love.

The way in which we describe death will depend on our own beliefs, but we have to remember that children are matter-of-fact thinkers. It does nothing to soften the blow if we use such expressions as 'gone to sleep'; 'gone to heaven'; 'passed away'. They may know already that dead things are buried or burned and they will be able to accept that this is what happens to dead people, too, if we do not attempt to gloss over the fact.

## Answering their questions

When something touches them deeply and personally the questions children ask are among the most difficult for the adult to answer. None of us knows why death comes to someone young or healthy, nor do we know what happens after death has taken place.

I firmly believe that a background of Christian belief does much to comfort a child at this time. We are able to assure him that although we don't know why death has come to Mummy or Daddy or to some other member of the family, we do know that the love of God is unshakeable and holds us all, in life and in death, and that nothing can separate us from him.

This, of course, is far too abstract for a grieving child fully to take in, but in our own case I found that it was possible to illustrate this by pointing out that all the kindness, invitations, flowers and letters that we received were God's way of showing us his love—by sending other people to look after us.

# The child's mourning

To mourn is just as much a psychological necessity for the child as for the adult and cannot be rushed. He needs time to be sad, to remember, to work through the feelings of loneliness and loss. It may help him if he talks about his feelings so that he comes to understand what is going on inside him, and so can cope with his emotional conflict.

## Going to the funeral

It is natural to wish to spare children the ordeal of the funeral service, but we should think again. To be present and take part in this ritual exorcises many fears and helps the child, like the adult, to face the reality of death. However harrowing the sight of a grieving child may be, he *needs* to face the truth.

## Patterns of behaviour

Many children react to death with anti-social behaviour and aggressiveness, disguising their fear by demanding that everything should be all right again. The bereaved child may be hostile to other members of the family; he may be 'rude' or unnaturally noisy.

Generally speaking, children under the age of five appear to ignore the fact of death because it is beyond their understanding, though they will be well aware of the atmosphere of distress in the home and will respond with various anxiety symptoms, often becoming demanding and clinging. Between the ages of five and nine, they think of death as a punishment on them for their naughtiness and that, if they are 'good', the dead person will come back again — this is why it is important for this age group to attend the funeral and be helped to realize death's finality. It is not until they are ten or eleven that children understand death more fully.

Following the first shock and tears, there often follows a period of quiet despair. The child may become withdrawn and unable to concentrate on anything. As a result, his school work will suffer. He needs reassurance that this is perfectly normal and is nature's way of giving him a rest until he is strong enough to take the strain. We have to judge when the time has come to nudge him out of himself once more.

## Helping the child recover

By talking to the children and giving them plenty of time to talk to us, we help each other. In times of grief, habit is a great help and children should go to school as usual and be encouraged to do jobs about the house. This will give them a renewed sense of purpose.

Schools can play a vital part. In these days, there will almost certainly be several other children at school with only one parent. Although insensitive and cruel in other ways, children treat a bereaved friend much more kindly and naturally than the adult world treats the bereaved parent. In my experience, teachers, too, go out of their way to support the child, and should always be told what has happened, especially if exams are looming.

## Outside help

Although the family should not shut itself away, we should be wary about accepting invitations on the children's behalf too soon after the death. Balance is essential — at first, we shall all be tempted to stay indoors in miserable isolation. Many teenagers, however, will feel that their entire social life has been cut off. It is important for them to emerge as soon as they feel able to cope with the inevitable curious looks and attempts to take their minds off it.

With younger children it can be counter-productive to push them out against their will. We must decide carefully whether they need protecting a little longer or whether they should be given a gentle push. One solution is to encourage their friends into *your* home. This will also be good for you: it will now be more necessary than ever to keep up with youthful attitudes and ideas to bring up a family single-handed.

# The one-parent family

# Adaptation

Bringing up children single-handed is hard work and there is no virtue in trying to be independent and going it alone. People are willing to lend a hand, and organizations exist to help and advise. Many men will be glad to take fatherless boys to a football match, or even on holiday with their own family. Neighbours and friends will sometimes offer to take children shopping, or to a show or concert. It is both rude and stupid to refuse such kindnesses.

## Parents' roles

It very quickly becomes obvious that it is impossible for anyone to be both mother and father. Losing a parent means that the family *is* incomplete and all its members have to learn to live within the new limitations. However, I tried to take an intelligent interest in my sons' passions. I began to watch televised football *with* them and found I was becoming interested myself. Children have an innate sense of fair play and the boys co-operated by entering into *my* hobbies, offering advice on knitting patterns or designs— and always ready with food suggestions!

## Where to go for help

Not every single-parent family is surrounded by good friends and neighbours. Not all bereaved adults are able to cope. The parent often feels isolated and alone with his problems, but several organizations exist to give advice and practical help.

# Looking forward

Sometimes the parent will involve the children in a family decision, to raise their drooping self-confidence. But as they grow up, they may turn to others outside the family to discuss some problem they would rather not talk about to us.

We must not resent this; our main concern is that they grow up wisely, no matter who helps them do so. Our task is to supply the security they need to enter into the full life which is their birthright as children of God. There must never be pressure on a child to stay at home to keep mother or father company. We bring up children solely to equip them to leave us, free and independent.

## Remarriage

Freedom is also *our* right—we may remarry, and if we have taught our children respect for individual freedom, they will understand. Provided that we and our children have 'let go' of the dead parent, this new relationship can be welcomed and entered into with hope. Reassure the children that to remarry is not disloyal to the previous partner, nor does it mean they are forgotten.

## Closer family life

Any study of one-parent families is bound to be depressing. But most families *do* survive—not unmarked, but with scars that heal. Families with a forward-looking approach and a faith to carry them along have the best chance.

Bereavement *can* result in closer family intimacy. Discipline can be simpler when there is only one parent, and in the new atmosphere of mutual concern you can explain why certain things are not allowed. The generation gap can be bridged: when you have seen each other with defences down and deep feelings expressed, such difficult subjects as sex, politics and religion become easier to discuss.

## New achievements

In a newspaper article, a lone father put his own hopeful views. He said, 'The one-parent family only survives if it pulls together. I used to tell my daughters, "Put into it as much as you take out." ' He got to know his children thoroughly. He felt a sense of achievement in looking after each child properly. It gave an extra dimension to his life. He thinks his daughters also benefitted, later on, when they had to make their own decisions.

# How can others help?

After a death, everyone wants to help but doesn't know how to. It isn't easy to know, because the persons bereaved will usually be unable to decide what they want. They need time to take in what has happened, and in the meantime practical help.

---

My dear Paul,

We have just heard the sad news. I know you have your family with you, but if there is anything we can do to help, you know you have only to ask.

Words are little help at a time like this and so I won't burden you with a long letter, but simply assure you that we are thinking of you and praying that God will comfort and strengthen you all in these sad days.

With our deepest sympathy and our love,

Mary and John

---

Unless there has been a definite request for 'no letters' (see page 7), a note of sympathy can bring a warm touch of comfort. It should be brief and should not refer to any other matter. Don't worry about what to say—provided you write from the heart, you will strike the right note. This is no time to be formal.

## Help from the family

The family is the obvious source of help, but not all families are dependable. Some people will have no family at all, and many other families are widely scattered. Nevertheless, however seldom they meet and whatever the tensions between them, at the time of bereavement they can be a source of great comfort and solidarity in the face of an uncertain future. As a widow said, 'I hadn't seen half of them for years but somehow it felt we were all close because we'd all lost one of the family.'

## Help from organizations

Many organizations have been set up to help the bereaved. Such clubs must be seen not as ends in themselves, but as stepping-stones between one stage of life and another. Otherwise, the danger is that they will become inward-looking and their members may feed on each other's fears and depressions instead of overcoming them. The organizations themselves recommend that their members leave once they feel strong enough. But in the early months many people are relieved to discover that they are not alone.

# Professional help

## The church

One of the first visitors to the bereaved family is likely to be a clergyman. Ministers say that this is a side of their work in which they feel most at a loss. The minister should not be disconcerted if the bereaved's faith seems shaken; it may be that he or she is having to ask questions for the first time. Nearly all the people I have spoken to agree that the clergyman who gave them most help was the one who recognized that there was nothing he could say to alter the *fact* of death but who in some way conveyed that they were not alone in their suffering.

On the other hand, the church *has* got something to say. A woman was grieving inconsolably for her husband, killed by a tractor. When the vicar came, she only said, 'Go away, you can't help me.' He put his hand on her head. 'I *can* help you,' he told her, 'I am here on God's behalf. I have his authority to bring you comfort and peace.'

## Medical help

Most people, however, now turn more naturally to the medical profession than to the church. Seventy-five per cent of bereaved people visit their doctor during the first six months after the death. Regrettably, only a few minutes can be allotted to each patient these days. But time is just what the bereaved person needs—he cannot marshall his thoughts to describe his symptoms and feelings adequately in five minutes.

The doctor, however, is often forced into prescribing sleeping-pills and tranquillizers, without the advice that should go with them. These drugs have their place, but more important by far is the listening ear, reassurance, and a promise that they can come to the surgery whenever they need to. Doctors also have to understand why angry words may be hurled at them—this is the urge of the bereaved to rationalize death and to find a scapegoat. The bereaved person needs confidence in the doctor to understand grief and its effects. Here, the doctor can help by pointing out that sometimes life *is* tragic, there are some things that *can't* be drugged away.

Health visitors and social workers who see bereaved people can help a great deal in providing moral support. They can tell a young widow it is natural that she finds the children difficult to cope with, while watching for any sign that the pressures are becoming too great. They can, above all, listen objectively, give a problem its own proportion, and give advice from their considerable experience.

# How friends can help

Try not to shower the bereaved man or woman with too much advice. Plans will have to be made, but the value of reliable, trustworthy friends lies in their willingness to listen, reassure and encourage. Add a little congratulation on the progress being made—this does much to raise spirits!

Pity is not helpful—it only leads to self-pity. What *is* needed is understanding compassion backed up by practical help. Keeping a home running smoothly, cooking meals, doing the laundry are huge burdens to an exhausted father or mother. Spontaneous and thoughtful acts of kindness will be much appreciated—a cake for tea, an offer to take the children to the park, an invitation for Sunday lunch. For six Sundays running after my husband died a good friend had us all to lunch and then allowed me to sleep all afternoon while her husband took the children out. It was those Sundays that kept us all sane!

## Visiting

Frequent short visits are more valuable than occasional long ones. They are a reminder that you are not forgotten. Visitors often find conversation difficult. This is understandable, because talking about things that must now appear trivial will seem wrong, and this rules out large areas of normal chat. As it is impossible to ignore what has happened, it is better to say right at the start how sorry you are. There can be no 'right' thing to say—the only way is to speak openly and warmly and take your cue from the other person's reaction. The same approach is needed when speaking to the children—this is a time when they must be treated like adults, with dignity.

Be prepared for anything, from laughter to tears. A friend can be just the person to confide in when members of the family may be too upset. You may be playing a most important part in the bereaved person's recovery.

## Long-term caring

Encourage them to pick up threads as soon as possible. Try to include them in normal activities—*not* just when you haven't anything better to do. And not only in the first few, dreadful weeks, but to go *on* caring, visiting and making the effort to see behind the answer 'Oh, I'm fine', when you ask them how they are. Months, even years, later there will be bad patches which can be worse than the first effects of grief. By sympathetically drawing them out you may be helping them over another hump.

It is important for friends not to be too forceful when giving their opinions; the bereaved person has little enough self-confidence and your apparently impregnable position will only injure it still more. Most people, given the chance to speak aloud about a problem, find it working itself out in their minds while they talk. Gentle encouragement and the suggestion of some side of it which may not have occurred to them may be all that is necessary.

Never try to force anyone to reveal their deepest feelings unless they want to—some are too personal or distressing. We have to distinguish between pity, which serves only to feed self-pity, and true comfort which strengthens. Genuine concern is what counts, plus the attempt to put yourself in their place: avoid the trite clichés which would drive you mad if they were said to *you*.

## Self-respect

The aim of all those wanting to help the bereaved should be to raise their dignity, self-respect and self-dependence. If there are very young children, an offer to baby-sit will be appreciated as most young widows cannot afford to pay and so find themselves spending every evening at home. A vague 'Let me know if I can do something' is rarely anything more than conventional politeness. It's best to decide on something which they *will* need help with—the washing, cooking or shopping—and offering to do that.

If the bereaved person has to ask for help on too many levels, it will only add to the general sense of inadequacy. A widow is usually reluctant to ask a friend's husband for help, fearing that his wife may suspect her motives. And make it sound as though you'd *like* to do the job—almost as though the bereaved person would be doing you a favour by allowing you to do it!

I remember having a dreadful cold and sitting looking at a basket overflowing with damp clothes when a friend dropped in, took everything in at a glance and said, 'Oh *do* let me do that ironing while we talk—I can't bear washing but I love ironing and I'd really enjoy it.' She was so convincing I still don't know whether it was true or not, but I was grateful!

Occasions like school prizegivings or sports days can bring acute anguish for the lone parent, not only because of the array of husbands and wives together but because you wish the children's father or mother could see them now. The support of another person close to the family can make all the difference. The children will be pleased that they are worth coming to see and the parent will not feel so much the odd one out.

## Common fears

Many people, especially women, may be frightened of going into an empty house after dark—or even in the daytime. If you have taken a friend home after a trip to the shops or an evening out, it really is a kindness to *insist* on going at least as far as the hall with them. There is nothing so forlorn as a silent, empty house and it is a relief to be helped over those first few minutes.

# Preparing for bereavement

I shall always be glad that my husband and I once discussed the inevitable fact that one of us would die before the other. Medical evidence shows that being prepared does help the bereaved person, and lessens the confusion which follows any death. Apart from the advantage of knowing where to turn for help, there will be the comfort of knowing what you decided together.

# Making a will

Both husband and wife should make a will even if there seems little of value to leave. Otherwise, when his wife dies, the husband won't know what she wanted to be done with her goods—and there will be needless legal problems.

To avoid legal pitfalls, it's best for a solicitor to draw up the will; this isn't very expensive. You simply make an appointment and take with you: (1) a list of your savings and belongings, with their value; (2) the names of two people who have agreed to act as executors (i.e. to distribute the belongings after your death); and (3) the names of the people you want to inherit your property, whether specific items or a proportion. The solicitor prepares the will, which you then sign with two witnesses present (they mustn't benefit under the will). It is best to let the solicitor keep the will safe, and for you to keep a copy at home with the solicitor's address.

## Children

Remember to make provision for any children, financially and for their upbringing. There is a possibility, however small, that the parents may both be killed, and so the will should say who is to be responsible for the children. You will need to get the people you choose as guardians to agree, of course. When considering who they should be, the interest of the *children* must come first. Some children worry about the possibility of their parents' dying; if they ask 'What will happen to us if you both die?' they can be reassured to know that Peter and Mary Brown, whom they know and trust, will look after them.

# Sorting out your affairs

## Your house

If you are buying your house, make sure that your life insurance is linked to the mortgage—it is essential to know that you will still have a roof over your head if your partner dies. If the house is already your own, discuss whether one partner can afford to live in it without the other. If you rent your home, is the lease in the husband's name only? If so, the wife may be given notice to quit. If the house is rented from the local council, you should find out how things operate in your area—phone them and ask. Some will transfer a tenancy, but some will ask you to find somewhere else to live—although they have to rehouse an existing tenant.

## Money and documents

Remember that it will be impossible to get any money under the terms of the will until the legal formalities have been completed (see pages 10-11). Try to ensure that somewhere (e.g. a joint

**Do you know where they are?**
Husband's will
Wife's will
Insurance policies
Bank passbooks
Building society passbooks
Birth certificates
Marriage certificates
National Savings certificates
Motor insurance certificate
Rent book
Cheque card
Credit cards
Driving licences
Television licence

bank account) there is a sum of money, however small, which the bereaved partner can call on to tide over the immediate demands. In times of stress, we do not think clearly and memories are faulty, so make sure you both know where all the important documents are kept which may have to be produced. You don't need to understand everything involved, but to have a grasp of the basics will make all the difference.

# Coping with serious illness

Sometimes death strikes without warning but more often there is a period of illness first. Although this is a harrowing time, it can be used in some degree to prepare the family for bereavement if it should come.

Life has changed; it has narrowed to visits to the hospital, long hours at the bedside. There is the feeling of panic and of resentment. Severe illness is an emotional drain for everyone, and it helps to recognize this and to adjust to living from one day to the next.

For Christians, it should be easier to discuss what is happening openly. If the sick person is still mentally aware, it can be a source of comfort to face the future together, drawing on the promises of God that life goes on after death and that his loving protection will embrace those left behind.

## Handling the situation

However feeble the patient may be, treat him normally, not like a baby. Try to understand his needs—if he wants to talk, let him; if he wants you to talk, do so calmly and normally.

Organize things so that at some period each day you can be by yourself to regain your sense of proportion. Don't be too hard on yourself—you won't be able to keep it up.

# Relationships

Another way to prepare for bereavement is to lead a full and friendly life. It is never good for a couple to be too self-sufficient and dependent on each other to the exclusion of other people. Old friendships should be kept up and new ones formed all the way through life. Then the loneliness of bereavement will be lessened by the care and concern of all sorts of people.

Children who are brought up in a home where people are always coming and going learn to be outgoing and friendly and to benefit from different outlooks and relationships.

and will find life much easier later on if they can sew on a button and press their jeans. It is to everyone's advantage if *all* the members of the family are taught how to drive the car, and so on.

## Sharing the work

Equality between the sexes means that the traditional roles of men and women are changing. These days, either may do the other's traditional work. So men should know how to use the washing-machine and change a nappy. Women should learn how to cope with minor electrical faults, decorate a room, etc.

Teach the children any jobs within their scope. Boys usually enjoy cooking

## Other work interests

As the children grow up, it is a good thing for wives to think over the practical and psychological advantages of brushing up their pre-marriage jobs or taking further training of some sort, in anything they would enjoy doing which would bring in money should the need arise. Even if they never have to support the family single-handed, such interests outside the home will help keep the marriage fresh and alive.